AF228283

The FORT RESTAURANT COOKBOOK

NEW FOODS OF THE OLD WEST FROM THE LANDMARK COLORADO RESTAURANT

HOLLY ARNOLD KINNEY
PHOTOGRAPHS BY LOIS ELLEN FRANK

An imprint of Globe Pequot, the trade division of
The Rowman & Littlefield Publishing Group, Inc.
4501 Forbes Blvd., Ste. 200
Lanham, MD 20706
www.TwoDotBooks.com

Distributed by NATIONAL BOOK NETWORK

British Library Cataloguing in Publication Information available

Library of Congress Cataloging-in-Publication Data

Names: Kinney, Holly Arnold, 1954- author.
Title: The Fort restaurant cookbook : new foods of the Old West from the landmark Colorado restaurant / Holly Arnold Kinney ; photographs by Lois Ellen Frank.
Description: Guilford, Connecticut : TwoDot, [2021] | Includes index. | Summary: "A celebration of the Fort restaurant in Morrison, CO, and many favorite recipes developed throughout its 56-year history"—Provided by publisher.
Identifiers: LCCN 2021009500 (print) | LCCN 2021009501 (ebook) | ISBN 9781493056354 (cloth) | ISBN 9781493056361 (epub)
Subjects: LCSH: Cooking, American—Western style. | Fort (Restaurant) | Cooking—Colorado. | LCGFT: Cookbooks.
Classification: LCC TX715.2.W47 K56 2021 (print) | LCC TX715.2.W47 (ebook) | DDC 641.59788—dc23
LC record available at https://lccn.loc.gov/2021009500
LC ebook record available at https://lccn.loc.gov/2021009501

∞™ The paper used in this publication meets the minimum requirements of American National Standard for Information Sciences—Permanence of Paper for Printed Library Materials, ANSI/NISO Z39.48-1992.

Acknowledgments

I WANT TO THANK my father, Samuel Paul Arnold ("Sam'l"), and my mother, Elizabeth Ann ("Bay") Arnold, for creating The Fort and me! The Fort not only has been my home since I was nine years old, but it sparked an adventure to last a lifetime! I'd also like to thank my husband, Jeremy F. Kinney, for insisting I purchase The Fort when my father put The Fort on the market in 1998. I purchased 49 percent and created a partnership with my father in 1999. In 2006, I purchased the land and his remaining interest after he passed in June 2006. Jeremy said, "It is your DESTINY! It's in your blood . . . you MUST do this!" Given his unconditional love and encouragement over 25 years, I'm so grateful that I married my soulmate!

I give a big-shout out to my past and present loyal Fort family of employees, who give shinin' times to our guests every night, since 1963! You are "Waugh-some!"

Thank you to my amazing Kiowa food photographer, Lois Ellen Frank, and Diné chef Walter Whitewater, whose eagle eye for detail, in front of and behind the camera, brought The Fort's recipes alive in this book. I'd also like to thank TwoDot and editor Erin Turner for producing a beautiful book that will be cherished by not only our guests, but the general public, who hunger for recipes inspired by our ancestors.

Contents

Shinin' Times at The Fort

THE FORT IS A VERY SPECIAL PLACE FOR ME, my family, everyone who works here, and our guests. When you walk through our impressively large, hand-carved wooden doors, you are overcome with a warm, magical feeling—something I have experienced since I was a small girl living above the restaurant on the mountain-rimmed plains outside Denver, Colorado.

The Fort is a full-scale replica of Bent's Fort, a well-known 19th-century fur-trading post in southwest Colorado. It's built of adobe, with its characteristic reddish-brown color that glimmers in the setting sun and beckons hungry diners. When my mother and father decided to build The Fort, they made sure to do so following age-old techniques for adobe buildings. Today, The Fort is on the National Register of Historic Places.

The Fort's Magic

Next to The Fort nestles a gigantic red rock. In the early 1960s, my mother told me that the rock was a spiritual magnet that created an aura that affected every person who came in range of it. When my parents scouted locations for the adobe home they planned to build, the rock drew them in with its intense spiritual energy and strength. It's a gorgeous red color that plays dramatically with our clear blue skies and vivid western sunsets.

The Fort and the rock became my home when I was just nine years old. While they were constructing The Fort, my mom and dad decided to turn the building into a restaurant, and we eventually moved into the top floor, which today holds the restaurant offices.

Since it opened in 1963, The Fort has welcomed hundreds of thousands of happy customers and its fair share of celebrities and dignitaries. In 1997, President Bill Clinton hosted an official Summit of Eight dinner there, celebrating the quintessentially American flavor of the locale and the food. The Crown Prince of Jordan recently had dinner with us, entertained by four-star generals from the Pentagon. Governor Bill Ritter and Denver mayor John Hickenlooper hosted several delegations during the 2008 Democratic Convention because, like Clinton before them, they appreciated the total experience of eating at The Fort. In the summer of 2019, Senator Cory Gardner brought the president of Taiwan, Tsai Ing-wen, and her delegation to The Fort for a luncheon. We had to find a petting zoo that had two horses, as President Tsai wanted to experience riding a horse in our fields below, with Senator Gardner, after her lunch at The Fort.

As thrilled as we are by such high-profile guests, our favorites are the loyal guests, many of them multigenerational, who have entered our doors since 1963. We hear from guests all the time about their own shinin' times at The Fort, whether it's a great dinner with family or friends, a holiday meal, or a joyful bar mitzvah or wedding.

We always have great fun at The Fort. Birthday celebrants are given a ceremonial headdress to wear; at Halloween the staff dresses in costumes; and in the 1960s and 70s, my pet bear, aptly named Sissy Bear, was known to saddle up to the bar for a bottle of soda pop.

The gentle bear "kissed" several celebrities and school-children, and she showed up in lots of photographs. We'll go to any length to ensure that dining with us gives our guests a memorable experience.

The Real Shinin' Star

As delightful as Sissy Bear was, our food is the real shinin' star at The Fort. The menu is based on the foods of the early 19th century, when fur traders roamed the region, often using Bent's Fort as their headquarters. That fort was operational from only 1833 to 1849, but in those short 16 years, it influenced much of the history of Colorado and the westward expansion of the United States. At our restaurant, as at Bent's Fort, game meat rules, especially buffalo, elk, and quail. Rest assured that our game dishes are prepared with the 21st-century palate very much in mind. We are true to the spirit of our American past. "New Foods of the Old West" is our motto.

Just as important as the dishes from Bent's Fort are those of the Native Americans who coexisted with the traders and mountain men. We serve Taos trout, buffalo boudies, medallions of elk, buffalo tongue, and buffalo marrow bones. Many of our dishes are based on the vegetables considered by Indians across the country as the three sacred sisters: corn, beans, and squash.

Our core menu of game and heritage dishes never changes, which is reassuring to guests who make a point of visiting us every time they are in Colorado, or who plan a once-a-year meal with us for a special occasion. Our talented chefs change other parts of the menu with the seasons, incorporating what is best and fresh from Colorado's farms and ranches, streams and woodlands. For limited times, dependent on supply, we also serve rattlesnake cakes made of snakes from Texas and musk ox raised by First Nations people in Canada.

On these pages you will find recipes from our standing menu as well as many others that have appeared from time to time, season to season, or for a very special occasion.

My Family, Our Family, Your Family

My family has always felt strongly about passing on recipes from one generation to the next. This is a way to preserve family traditions and link to our family histories. This conviction is true on both sides of the family. Bay, my mother, was from a Southern family that settled in Georgia in the early 1700s, and Sam'l, my father, was from an equally old Pennsylvania family. I am fortunate to have old notebooks and cookbooks from both families, and in this book you will find some of my favorite family dishes.

Both of my parents believed in family and culinary history, and so they collected historic and little-known cookbooks when they researched the food that would eventually be served at The Fort. Most of these books document recipes from the early 19th century in Mexico and the Southwest. I have inherited this invaluable library, which now boasts more than 2,000 volumes, many of which are extremely rare. My parents didn't collect all 2,000; many came from their own parents, but my father hired antiquarians to expand the collection so that, during a 50-year span, he acquired just about every book there was on his favorite subject.

Throughout this book, I often quote or paraphrase my dad. He was a respected historian and I found writing this book an exceptional opportunity to share his knowledge and research with an ever-wider audience. I learned a lot going back through his work, and I hope you will find it as fascinating as I do.

We celebrate all families at The Fort, not just mine. Because we welcome all families, large and small, many

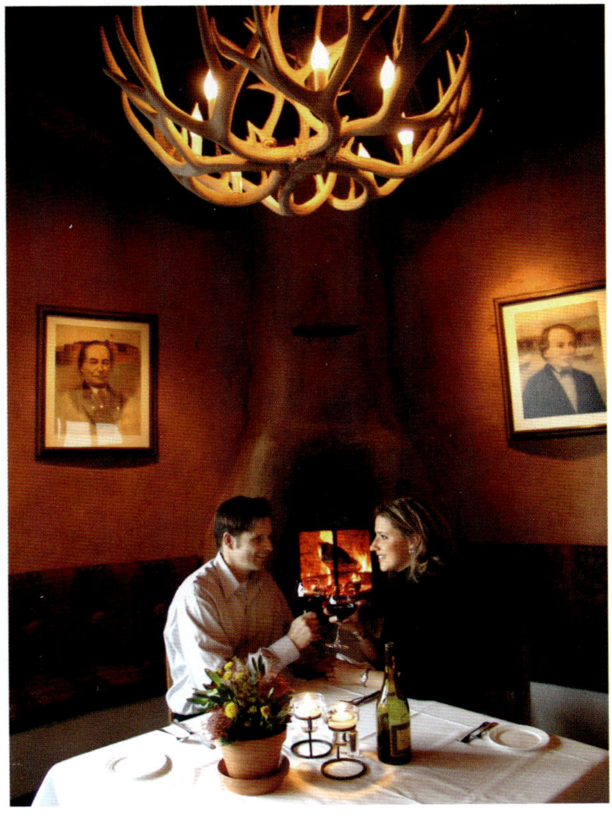

of our guests choose The Fort to celebrate birthdays, anniversaries, and other happy occasions. I call our customers "guests," as I consider each person a guest in my home, The Fort. I hope this book will be used by all members of your family. When I was a kid, my parents encouraged me to cook alongside them. Not only did I love the time I got to spend with them, but it gave me confidence in the kitchen. I hope you will do the same. I promise: the entire family will have some Fort-style shinin' times!

THE FORT

Beginners

Fort Guacamole

Our guests love our guacamole, and for good reason. It's been voted the best by Denver's *Westword* newspaper, but even without the accolade we know how truly spectacular it is. We make it the way it's traditionally made in Mexico, where it originated as a way to use overripe avocados. Mexican cooks stirred salsa cruda—made with fresh tomatoes, serrano chiles, and cilantro—into the avocados and a glorious dish was born. In most Mexican households, neither garlic nor lime juice is part of the mix, but cooks lay slices of fresh lime on top of the dip to prevent it from oxidizing and turning brown. At The Fort, we add lime juice but never, ever use garlic or cumin. Cumin is a big no-no in New Mexican cooking, a regional conceit we follow here.

SERVES 4–6

Ingredients

3 ripe Hass avocados, pitted and peeled

3 whole serrano chiles, seeded and minced

¼ cup freshly squeezed lime juice (2 small limes)

½ teaspoon salt

2 large, ripe tomatoes, seeded and diced

1 medium white onion, diced

¼ cup whole fresh cilantro leaves (no stems), minced

Directions

1. Place avocados, chiles, lime juice, and salt in a large bowl. Mash avocados with a fork or potato masher, leaving small lumps.

2. Gently fold in tomatoes, onion, and cilantro. Taste, and add more lime juice if desired. The guacamole should be spicy, so add more serrano chiles as your taste dictates. Serve with freshly fried corn tortilla chips.

WHEN A BEGINNER IS A BEGINNING

My father, Sam'l, called appetizers "beginners" because during the 1800s, that was a popular term for any small dish served before the main event. Why fool around with an unfamiliar word when an obvious one does just as well?

Our menu at The Fort offers a long list of beginners. Some have been there from the 1960s, while others were added as the years went by. I have introduced a few I particularly like and have found to be great favorites with our guests.

Hot Sausage Bean Dip

Back in the day, my dad and a group of chefs took an annual fishing trip to friend Fritz Covillo's cabin in Ouray, Colorado, high in the Rocky Mountains. Fritz always served a hot sausage dip that, as Dad said, was "so good as to make a grown man cry!" Since then, we have served a version of the dip at The Fort, and while we hope no one cries when they taste it, it's fantastic for any sort of celebration at any time of year. I especially like to make this during football season, and it's also great heated up over a hot, smoky campfire. At the restaurant, we use buffalo sausage, but use your favorite pork or poultry sausage if you prefer.

SERVES 8–10

Ingredients

2 pounds refried beans (two 16-ounce cans)

8 ounces dark beer

¾ pound buffalo sausage

¾ cup finely chopped white onion

3–5 serrano chiles, seeded and finely minced

1½–2 cups grated cheddar cheese

Directions

1. Heat the beans and beer in a double boiler to prevent burning.

2. Meanwhile, in a large sauté pan, brown sausage and onion over medium heat. Stir to crumble the sausage as it cooks. Pour off any fat and add the chiles. Sauté a few minutes longer, then combine with the bean and beer mixture.

3. At the last minute, stir in the cheese, which will melt nicely into the warm dip. Serve with fresh, warm corn tortillas.

Mountain Man Boudies

My father recognized how delicious these boudies were and made them whenever possible. They are a staple at The Fort, and we have any number of customers who cannot get enough of them. Sam'l wrote about their history: *During the fur-trade period, the American West was populated by many French-Canadians making their living as beaver trappers. A favorite food was boudin, or any type of sausage, preferably those similar to the blood sausage of France. The English word "pudding" originates from the French word boudin, and the recipe for boudin generally consisted of meat and some form of cereal cooked together and pushed into intestine casings. English-speaking mountain men couldn't pronounce "dem furrin languidges," so they simply called boudin "dem boudies."*

MAKES 12 SAUSAGES; SERVES 6

Ingredients

1 cup hulled sunflower seeds

3 pounds buffalo round, brisket, or plate

¼ pound buffalo, beef, or pork fat (see Note)

1 cup uncooked instant oatmeal

2 yellow onions, finely chopped

1½ tablespoons coarsely ground black pepper

1 tablespoon chile caribe (coarsely ground red chile)

2 cups dried breadcrumbs

1½ teaspoons ground sage

1½ teaspoons dried thyme

1½ teaspoons dried leaf oregano

1½ tablespoons whole cumin seed

10 feet large pork casings (optional)

Directions

1. Toast sunflower seeds in a small skillet over medium-low heat, stirring until lightly browned, 3 to 5 minutes. Allow to cool.

2. Fit the meat grinder with the chile plate and grind the buffalo meat with the fat. Put the mixture through the meat grinder again, so that the meat is ground twice.

3. Combine the ground meat mixture with the remaining ingredients, oatmeal through cumin seed. With a sausage stuffer, fill the pork casings to make individual boudies twisted off every 6 inches. If you don't want to bother with casings, simply shape the mixture into patties.

4. Grill the links or patties over medium-hot coals for 3 to 5 minutes per side. They can also be cooked on a griddle or in a greased pan. To be true to history, the boudies would be boiled and served hot. At The Fort, boudies in casings are boiled ahead of time, then grilled.

5. After they are boiled, boudies in casings keep very well in the freezer. When you want to eat them, defrost in the refrigerator, then grill or cook them on a griddle as indicated above. If you make patties, freeze them raw, then defrost and grill or cook on a griddle.

Note: The fat around the kidneys is the purest, so ask the butcher for it when you order the fat. You can also ask the butcher to grind the meat and fat for you. If you would rather not use fat, use 3¼ pounds of lean beef and put it through the grinder twice.

SAUSAGE MAKING

Early journals from the West tell of dicing prime parts of buffalo, salting and peppering them, adding a little onion and cornmeal and likely some red chile pepper, and then stuffing the mixture into a length of buffalo gut that had been cleaned and turned inside out, so that any fat was on the outside. The sausages were tied off with a whang (a short piece of rawhide) and then either broiled over the fire or boiled in a big pot. References to this culinary feat written in 1830s more often call for boiling rather than broiling.

Today, it's a lot easier to make sausage, although not too many home cooks attempt it. Heavy-duty stand mixers, such as KitchenAids, are fitted with attachments for grinding and filling casings that make short work of the process. If you don't want to stuff the meat mixture into casings, you can always form it into patties and pan cook them.

It is important to grind the meat for boudies coarsely. We grind it twice through the chile plate, which has larger holes than the plate used for most ground meat. If you don't have a machine, ask your butcher to grind the meat for you.

Buffalo Empanadas

We only recently added these empanadas to our menu, when former Chef Geoffrey Groditski developed them to honor the memory of his grandmother. According to Chef, she made the best empanadas ever and so he produced these light, flaky pastries filled with buffalo meat and served with two sauces. The minute they were on the menu, the empanadas were an instant hit. You cannot eat just one!

MAKES 18 EMPANADAS; SERVES 6

Ingredients

1½ tablespoons canola oil, plus more for frying

¾ cup chopped yellow onion

3 Anaheim chiles, roasted, peeled, and diced, or ½ cup canned mild green chiles

¾ pound lean ground buffalo

1 tablespoon minced fresh garlic (2 cloves)

4 teaspoons dried Mexican oregano

4 teaspoons medium-strength New Mexican chile powder (Dixon preferred)

1½ teaspoons ground cumin

1½ teaspoons ancho chile powder

Salt and freshly ground pepper, to taste

1–2 tablespoons all-purpose flour

1 (17⅓-ounce) package frozen puff pastry sheets, thawed

¾ cup of cheese shredded cheddar cheese

New Mexican Dixon Red Chile Sauce (page 60), for dipping

Chipotle BBQ Sauce (page 67), for dipping

Directions

1. Place 1½ tablespoons of oil in a large skillet over medium heat. Add onion and cook until translucent, 4 to 5 minutes. Add chiles, buffalo, garlic, and spices. Continue to cook, stirring, until meat loses its pink color and chiles have softened, about 10 minutes. Season meat mixture to taste with salt and pepper and set aside to cool.

2. On a lightly floured surface, roll puff pastry sheets to about ⅛-inch thickness. Using a 4-inch cutter, cut 9 rounds out of each sheet. If needed, reroll pastry scraps after stacking them and gently pressing together. Refrigerate pastry rounds, removing a few at a time to form empanadas.

3. Preheat the oven to 300°F. Place 1 rounded tablespoon of the meat mixture and about 1½ teaspoons of cheese on each puff pastry round. Moisten edges of dough with water, and fold in half to enclose filling. Use the tines of a fork to decoratively seal the edges. Empanadas may be refrigerated or frozen at this point.

4. Deep-fry empanadas in small batches at 375°F or panfry them in ½ inch of hot oil in a cast-iron skillet, turning occasionally, until golden brown. Drain empanadas on crumpled paper towels and keep warm in oven until all have been fried. Serve with one or both of the chile sauces.

Buffalo Eggs

This beginner at The Fort is made with tiny, pickled quail eggs wrapped in spicy buffalo sausage and then deep-fried. It's our version of Scotch eggs, and it's served with a tangy sauce that completes the dish as beautifully as hollandaise does eggs Benedict. Quail eggs are more full-flavored than chicken eggs and have the added benefit of being easy to pop in your mouth whole.

SERVES 6

Ingredients

Canola oil, for deep-frying

1 dozen pickled quail eggs (jarred, not canned) or 1 dozen small, hard-cooked hen eggs

1¾ pounds buffalo sausage or bulk hot Italian sausage

½–¾ cup all-purpose flour

½–¾ cup milk

1½–2 cups crushed white or yellow corn tortilla chips

Sweet Red Pepper Chili Sauce (page 57), for serving

Directions

1. Heat the deep-fryer oil to 350°F and the oven to 300°F.

2. Rinse the eggs and pat them dry. If you are using hen eggs, cut them in half, either lengthwise or crosswise.

3. Divide the sausage in half and roll or pat it out on a floured surface to a ⅜-inch thickness. (If you have enough counter space, don't bother dividing it.) Wrap each egg with enough sausage to completely cover the egg, then roll it in flour, dip in milk, and roll in tortilla crumbs.

4. Fry a few at a time until golden brown, 4 to 6 minutes. Drain the eggs on crumpled paper towels and keep them warm the preheated oven. Allow the frying oil to return to 350°F between batches. Serve with Sweet Red Pepper Chile Sauce.

Duck Quesadillas

The smoked duck filling is the result of two of our chefs perfecting a dish that has become a signature of the restaurant. Former executive chef Dave Woolley created a tasty barbecued, coffee-smoked duck filling in 2002 that he mixed with aged Mexican cheese before filling the quesadillas. Our current executive chef added his own touches for rehearsal dinners or weddings, and I have found the quesadillas to be perfect for cocktail parties of any kind. My husband, Jeremy, and I like a few for dinner with nothing more than a fresh green salad.

SERVES 4–8

Ingredients

DUCK

1 whole duck, approximately 5 pounds

2 quarts chicken broth

1 carrot, peeled and chopped

1 celery rib, chopped

½ yellow onion, sliced

3 cloves garlic, peeled and crushed with side of knife

2–3 bay leaves

¾ cup Coffee BBQ Sauce (page 65)

QUESADILLAS

8 eight-inch flour tortillas

2⅔ cups duck mixture

3 cups shredded panela or Monterey Jack cheese

Directions

1. Preheat the oven to 350°F.

2. Remove giblets and neck from the duck and reserve for another use. Rinse the duck inside and out with cold water and place it in a braising pan. Cover with broth, and add carrot, celery, onion, garlic, and bay leaves. Cover the pan tightly with a lid or aluminum foil. Place in the oven and braise for about 2 hours, until the duck is cooked through and tender.

3. Remove duck from the braising liquid and cut it into quarters. Smoke the quarters with hickory for 20 minutes. (See "Where to Find It!" or search online for retailers of foil smoking bags for use in home ovens.) After smoking, allow the duck to rest for about 10 minutes. Remove the skin and discard it. Remove meat from the bones and finely chop it. Mix the chopped duck with Coffee BBQ Sauce.

4. Place a flour tortilla on a medium-hot griddle. Top with ⅓ cup duck mixture and ⅓ cup cheese. Remove from the griddle when the tortilla is slightly crispy, and fold it in half. Cut into triangles and serve with your favorite salsa and crema or sour cream.

12 Shooters of Acapulco Shrimp

This easy shrimp beginner is the outcome of a trip Sam'l and Dave Woolley, who at the time was our executive chef, took to Mexico in 2003 with Rick Bayless. Rick is the owner of several Mexican restaurants in Chicago and is recognized as one of our nation's leading authorities on the cooking of that sunny land, and both Dad and Dave were excited about the journey. When they returned home, they were itching to add a shrimp ceviche made with bay shrimp, avocado, celery, and serrano chiles to The Fort's menu. I came up with the idea of turning the ceviche into shooters, served in shot glasses on a wooden plank with tortilla chips. At The Fort, you can down your two shooters and shout "Huzzah!"

MAKES 12 SHOOTERS; SERVES 6 (TWO SHOOTERS EACH)

Ingredients

SHRIMP

1 pound small shrimp, cooked and peeled (see Note)

1 cup diced celery

2 ripe avocados, peeled, pitted, and cut into 1-inch cubes

SAUCE

½ cup mayonnaise

1 ¼ cups tomato juice

1 tablespoon plus 1 teaspoon ketchup

2 teaspoons prepared horseradish

½ serrano chile, seeded and minced

6–8 cilantro leaves

Juice of 1 lime (3–4 tablespoons)

Dash of Worcestershire sauce

GARNISH

3–4 tablespoons small capers, drained (optional)

12 sprigs cilantro

12 lime slices

Directions

1. Rinse the shrimp in very cold water. Combine the shrimp and celery; this can be done well ahead of time. Add the avocado at the last minute to keep it from becoming discolored.

2. Combine mayonnaise, tomato juice, ketchup, horseradish, minced chile, cilantro leaves, lime juice, and Worcestershire in a blender or food processor. Pulse on and off, making sure the mayonnaise is fully incorporated.

3. When ready to serve, toss the sauce with the shrimp, celery, and avocado. Spoon into shot glasses and garnish each glass with a few capers, a sprig of cilantro, and a slice of fresh lime.

Note: We use Icelandic bay shrimp, but any quality shrimp will work. Try to choose fresh shrimp, rather than frozen.

Crispy Citrus Lamb Riblets

When Dad hungered for crispy lamb ribs, also known as Denver ribs, he asked Chef Dave Woolley to create a recipe for them. Dave spiced the ribs with a buffalo wing–style sauce, and today these little riblets are one of our most popular beginners. The Colorado Lamb Council features them often, too. Because lamb riblets are sometimes hard to find, I suggest you try these with baby back pork ribs. You won't be disappointed.

SERVES 4–6

Ingredients

RIBS

1½ racks (about 18 ribs) lamb spareribs or baby back pork ribs

2 large carrots, diced

2 celery stalks, diced

2 medium onions, diced

8 cups chicken broth

Canola oil for deep-frying

SAUCE

½ cup hot sauce (Frank's RedHot Sauce preferred)

⅓ cup Thai sweet red chili sauce (Mae Ploy preferred)

2 teaspoons tamarind syrup or Worcestershire sauce

2 teaspoons honey

⅛–¼ teaspoon tangerine oil

TOPPING

Black sesame seeds

Chopped cilantro

Chopped Italian parsley

Directions

1. Preheat the oven to 400°F. Place ribs, carrots, celery, onions, and chicken broth in a shallow roasting pan. Cover tightly with lid or aluminum foil and place pan on middle rack of the oven. Reduce heat to 325°F and braise the ribs for 2 hours or until tender.

2. Remove ribs from the liquid and allow to cool. With a sharp knife cut the rack into individual ribs and pat them dry with paper towels.

3. In a saucepan combine hot sauce, Thai sweet chili sauce, tamarind syrup, honey, and tangerine oil. Warm the sauce over medium heat, stirring occasionally, until heated through.

4. In a deep fryer, heat oil to 350°F. Fry the cooked ribs, in small batches, for 3 to 5 minutes, until browned and crisp.

5. Remove the ribs from the oil and drain them on a wire rack. While the ribs are still hot, toss with sauce. Sprinkle black sesame seeds, chopped parsley, and chopped cilantro on top. Serve immediately.

Roasted Buffalo Marrow Bones

At The Fort, we have been serving roasted buffalo marrow bones for more than 35 years. Both Julia Child and famed Italian chef Lidia Bastianich ordered the marrow bones as an appetizer and savored every bite. Most of our guests who have the curiosity to try it order it again and again.

When my dad, Sam'l, who was a respected food historian, first read about buffalo marrow bones in his research, he talked to our buffalo suppliers and convinced them to cut the knobs off the femurs (the front legs), split the bones in half, and sell them to us. Once they are cooked, we sprinkle them with a little Hawaiian clay finishing salt and serve them stacked like Lincoln Logs. Paul McIlhenny, of the Tabasco company family, was a good friend who suggested we put a few drops of Tabasco's green jalapeño sauce on the roasted marrow bones. We were sold as soon as we tasted the combination. This is an amazingly popular beginner at The Fort, and I eat it whenever I can. It is an incomplete protein and an unsaturated fat. It is supposed to be very good for your immune system.

SERVES 4–6

Ingredients

4–6 buffalo or beef femur bones

1 baguette

1 tablespoon olive oil

Hawaiian red clay sea salt or other coarse finishing sea salt

Cilantro sprigs or Italian parsley, for garnish

Tabasco Green Pepper Sauce (optional)

Directions

1. Saw the femur bones in half lengthwise or cut them into 1½-inch-thick disks. You might want to ask the butcher to do this for you.

2. Preheat the oven to 450°F. Arrange marrow bones on a jelly roll pan or baking sheet with sides and roast on the middle shelf of the oven for about 14 minutes. Watch the marrow as it cooks; you want it to remain gelatinous in the center. If overcooked, the marrow will liquefy.

3. While the bones are roasting, thinly slice the bread, brush the slices lightly with olive oil, and arrange them on a separate baking sheet. Place in the oven for about 5 minutes, until lightly toasted.

4. Arrange the marrow bones on oval serving plates. A sprinkling of Hawaiian red clay sea salt around the plate is very tasty and represents the Hawaiian fur traders hired by the American Fur Trade Company in the 1820s. Garnish with sprigs of cilantro.

5. Remove marrow from the bones with marrow spoons (available at many antique stores) or butter knives. Spread the marrow on the toasted bread. If desired, top with a dash of green pepper sauce.

AN ODE TO BUFFALO

Buffalo, or bison, as they are also called, have roamed our continent for tens of thousands of years. Ancestors of today's bison existed nearly 120,000 years ago; by the time the first Europeans arrived in the 1600s, estimates are that there were upwards of 60 million buffalo living in what today is North America.

The Plains tribes relied on the animals for food, clothes, shelter, and trade, and before the Spanish, French, and Americans brought guns, the Indians had any number of ways to kill enough bison to satisfy their needs. They used arrows, of course, but also would drive a herd off a cliff. The indigenous people respected the buffalo, admiring its strength, intelligence, speed, and character, and they believed that anyone who ate the flesh of the animals would gain some of the same attributes. Not surprisingly, Native Americans developed a number of rituals surrounding the killing of these magnificent animals and always honored the source of food for the tribe.

Between 1830 and 1860, nearly all the buffalo were slaughtered by Americans trying to meet the hunger for bison hides and bison tongues in Europe and the eastern states. Thousands upon thousands of bison were killed, some for profit and many for sport, so that, sadly, by the 1890s barely 300 buffalo were left. That they were nearly extinct troubled President Theodore Roosevelt a few years later and prompted him to urge Congress to establish wildlife preserves. Gradually and with careful husbandry, our bison herds have flourished so that today there is a sustainable number of bison. There are over 400,000 raised in commercial private herds as well as in parks. Many Indian tribes are raising buffalo today to reestablish healthy eating habits on the reservations.

In the 1840s, when some young adventurous Americans traveled the Santa Fe Trail from St. Louis to New Mexico, the buffalo were a common theme in personal diaries. Seventeen-year-old Lewis Garrard kept such a diary in 1846 that later became a book called *Wah-to-yah and the Taos Trail*.

"We never eat but twice a day, very often but once in 24 hours, at which scarcity of food, of course, there was grumbling," writes Garrard. "Darn this way of living, anyhow; a feller starves a whole day like a mean coyote and when he does eat, he stuffs himself like a snake that's swallowed a frog and is no account for an hour after."

After experiencing his first buffalo hunt, Garrard watched the more experienced men skin and butcher a "fine fat young male." He observed that the men ate the liver raw. "[They ate it] with a slight dash of gall by way of zest, which, served á la Indian, was not very tempting to cloyed appetites; but to hungry men, not at all squeamish, raw warm liver with raw marrow was quite palatable. Before the buffalo range was half traversed, I liked the novel dish pretty well!"

Other accounts describe "prairie butter," which is broiled buffalo bone marrow. This was considered a delicacy. Trappers and hunters took the hip and leg bones of the buffalo, split them, and roasted the marrow over the campfire. They sopped it up with good, hot sourdough bread, which explains why they called it butter.

Both Indians and trappers considered marrow an important food. While it usually was spread over bread, it also was used in soups and stews, and some frontier desserts included marrow with berries.

Europeans have long treasured beef marrow and these days Americans are recognizing its succulence. It's showing up at the best restaurants in New York, Chicago, and Los Angeles— and buffalo marrow has been on the menu at The Fort for years.

Rattlesnake Cakes

The rattlesnake meat we serve at The Fort is USDA inspected and comes from Texas (see "To Cook a Rattlesnake" on page 16), and because it's a seasonal meat, it's not always available. My dad created a recipe for these cakes, which are very similar in taste and texture to crab cakes. If you can find rattlesnake meat, you will love these, but they are also good made with chicken.

MAKES 12 CAKES; SERVES 6

Ingredients

1½ pounds boneless rattlesnake fillet or skinless, boneless chicken breasts

¾ cup finely diced red bell pepper

½ cup finely diced red onion

1½ tablespoons olive oil

¼ cup mayonnaise

2 large eggs

2 tablespoons fresh lime juice

⅓ cup panko breadcrumbs

1½ teaspoons kosher salt

¾ teaspoon ground cumin

½ teaspoon freshly ground black pepper

½ teaspoon ground Dixon chile (or other medium-heat New Mexican chile)

6 tablespoons clarified butter (see Note)

Directions

1. Steam rattlesnake (or chicken) in a steamer for 30 to 45 minutes, rotating it every 15 minutes to ensure even cooking. Snake should be firm but not hard to the touch when done. Allow to cool.

2. Place meat in food processor with a very sharp blade. Pulse two to three times, until it reaches a crab flake consistency. Do not process too long or the cakes will be mealy when done.

3. Sauté bell pepper and onion in olive oil until all moisture evaporates. Place the vegetables on a sheet pan to cool.

4. Combine panko and spices in a large mixing bowl. Set aside.

5. Place mayonnaise in a mixing bowl and whisk in eggs one at a time. Add lime juice and whisk until mixture is smooth.

6. Stir cooled vegetables, mayonnaise mixture, and chopped meat into panko and spices. Press the mixture into a 9-inch square pan, cover with plastic wrap, and chill in the refrigerator for at least 1 hour.

7. Form mixture into cakes using a 2-inch round biscuit cutter. Mixture must be tightly compressed to hold its form during cooking. Each cake should be about 1 inch thick when finished.

8. Preheat the oven to 400°F.

9. In a large skillet, over medium-high heat, sauté the cakes in clarified butter until they are golden brown, 2 to 3 minutes per side. Transfer cakes to a cookie sheet lined with baking parchment and finish in the oven, about 5 minutes.

Note: Clarified butter has had the milk solids removed and so keeps about three times longer as other butter. It's great for cooking because it can be heated to relatively high temperatures. To make it, melt about 1 cup (or more—but not less) of unsalted butter over low heat and let it simmer for about 20 minutes. Do not stir it during this time, during which moisture will evaporate and the white milk solids will sink to the bottom of the pan. Carefully pour the butter from the pan and leave the milk solids behind. (You can use a sieve if you prefer.) The clarified butter will be clear and richly golden. Use right away or let the butter cool and refrigerate for up to 3 months.

TO COOK A RATTLESNAKE

My father first cooked rattlesnake in 1975 at a festival in Historic Denver, where he also prepared more than 4,000 buffalo burgers and 300 pounds of Rocky Mountain oysters. He had 120 pounds' worth of rattlesnake, which he cut into chunks and dipped in tempura batter before deep-frying them. Delicious!

When I was about nine years old and had recently moved to The Fort, my older brother, Keith, and I caught a four-foot-long rattler down the hill from the restaurant. We killed it and brought it home with plans to skin it and make hat bands, as our mother had shown us. That evening a customer complained that we had no rattlesnake on the menu. We had buffalo and other game, he said, but no snake. My brother, who was bussing tables nearby, ran to fetch our trophy. He held the long, bloody creature in front of the customer and asked him which section he would like. We called his bluff and didn't have to cook the rattlesnake, but we did get some pretty cool hat bands that always reminded us of our catch.

Nowadays, rattlesnake is sometimes on our menu when it's in season. We get the boned snake meat primarily from Texas, where folks in the western part of the state participate in rattlesnake roundups. It seems that every so often, Texans get together to collect the numerous snakes slithering hither and yon on the prairie and turn the event into a contest, with prizes awarded for the longest, heaviest, and oldest snakes—or similar. Once the snakes are rounded up, meat purveyors take over.

We used to get the snakes skinned, heads removed, and frozen. They were tightly coiled, and when the cold snakes were submerged in boiling water, they unwound; some of our younger cooks feared they were coming to life!

My dad had a thing or two to say about rattlesnakes—of course! Here they are:

"Let them eat snake!" yelled the host of a small dinner party one night at The Fort. Much to his own amusement, the dish was brought to his table. For years, The Fort served a rattlesnake cocktail when it was in season. Today, we make a rattlesnake cake, similar to a crab cake. Each night, our guests ask for rattlesnake. If it isn't in season, and we don't have it, they are sorely disappointed. It is truly delicious.

The longest snake I ever saw was 76 inches long, but in New Mexico there are stories of much larger snakes. The larger, the better, as you can feed more guests. If you have caught a rattler and want to prepare it for cooking, first cool it in the refrigerator or freezer. It will go to sleep and will be safe to handle. Using a cleaver, or hatchet, cut off the head low enough down on the neck so that it may be freeze-dried and made into a hat ornament. Next, stretch it out on a table and, using a razor blade, an X-Acto knife, or a very sharp skinning knife, slice the skin of the belly lengthwise, starting at the neck and continuing down the snake. Remove the organs and wash well under running water. Use a pair of pliers to pull off the skin. It should be easy to remove since there is some fat between the skin and the muscle. Try not to damage the skin, for it may be rubbed on the underside with a little salt and then stretched onto a board and tacked down to dry for display as a monument to your bravery and culinary skills.

Once the snake is cleaned and skinned, braise it in a pot with the onion, bay leaf, and peppercorns. After 90 minutes of gentle boiling, the snake is done. Allow to cool, and then strip the meat from the bones by hand. Arrange atop of a bed of lettuce, on a serving platter or in cocktail glasses, and serve with a sweet red chile sauce.

There are many rattlesnakes around The Fort and up on our Red Rock, so be careful walking around. We want to be sure you bite the snake before he bites you!

Buffalo Tongue with Caper Sauce

I can still recall boiling buffalo tongue in water and Bays spices in the kitchen of The Fort with my mother. Even as a young girl, I was surprised at how large the tongues were but, even so, I realized they were smaller than beef tongue. After we boiled them, my mom and I peeled off the outer skin so that the tongues were edible. I was always taught to revere the buffalo tongue, which was considered sacred meat by the Indians and used in religious ceremonies. I was told to be grateful to the intelligent animal who sacrificed his life to nourish our stomachs and our souls.

My dad, Sam'l, wrote about the history of the buffalo tongue: *Buffalo tongue was thought by many to be the greatest gourmet delicacy of the American 19th century. Considered holy meat by Native Americans, it has a delicate flavor and fine texture and is far superior to beef tongue, which has a coarser quality. The demand for buffalo tongue was a major reason for the wholesale slaughter of the bison. Tragically whole herds were killed for their hides and tongues, the latter of which were smoked, salted, or pickled and sent east in fully loaded railroad cars. Such fine restaurants as Delmonico's in New York City reportedly served it to the likes of President Ulysses S. Grant and singer Jenny Lind, the Swedish Nightingale. Today, in limited numbers, buffalo tongues are once again gracing gourmet palates, for in addition to the herds that still roam on federally protected land, bison are thriving on ranches in all 50 states.*

SERVES 8–12

Ingredients

TONGUE

1 small yellow onion, coarsely chopped

1 bay leaf

1 tablespoon freshly ground black pepper

1 buffalo tongue (about 2 pounds)

CAPER SAUCE

1 cup mayonnaise

1 tablespoon capers, drained

1 tablespoon prepared horseradish

⅛ teaspoon dried oregano

¾ teaspoon freshly ground black pepper

Italian parsley, for garnish

Directions

1. Bring a large pan of water to a boil with the onion, bay leaf, and pepper. Add the tongue and reduce heat to low. Poach gently for 2½ to 3 hours, until tender and cooked through.

2. In a mixing bowl, whisk mayonnaise, capers, horseradish, oregano, and pepper until well blended. Cover and chill the sauce until ready to serve.

3. When the tongue is cooked, remove it from the poaching liquid and allow it to cool slightly. While it is still warm, peel off the light outer skin with a knife.

4. Preheat the broiler. Slice the tongue into ½-inch-thick pieces across the grain. Assemble on an ovenproof platter and heat briefly under the broiler. Place a bowl of the caper sauce on the platter and garnish with parsley.

Rocky Mountain Oysters with Panko

Even as a little girl, I worked in The Fort's kitchen as a prep cook. Peeling and cleaning Rocky Mountain oysters was a routine job, and I barely gave it a second thought. One day I invited my sixth-grade school friends to The Fort and before they arrived, I prepared a large bowl of lightly seasoned, deep-fried Rocky Mountain oysters. "These are delicious! What kind of sausage popcorn is this?" one friend asked as she and the others happily downed the little tidbits.

"You are eating buffalo bull testicles with a light breading and salt and pepper," I answered. They looked at me with disbelief but didn't stop munching them, and to this day, they still tell this story with much delight. Now they bring their friends and children to The Fort and surprise them with the same dish ordered off our menu. Calf fries—another name for testicles—are smaller and more tender than bull fries, so ask your butcher for them.

SERVES 6

Ingredients

6 calf or veal testicles (turkey testicles may be substituted)

1 cup panko breadcrumbs

1 teaspoon black pepper

¼ teaspoon cayenne (ground red pepper)

½ teaspoon salt

Canola oil for deep-frying

Sweet Red Chile Sauce (page 57), for dipping

Directions

1. With a sharp paring knife, cut and peel the skin away from the testicles. They will peel and slice much more easily if they are slightly frozen.

2. Cut the testicles into 1-inch pieces and pat them dry. In a shallow baking pan, combine the panko, black pepper, cayenne, and salt and roll the testicle pieces in this mixture. .

3. Heat oil to 375°F and preheat the oven to 200°F. Fry the breaded "oysters" for 3 minutes, until a light crust forms. Drain them on crumpled paper towels and keep them warm in the oven. If you are serving them as an appetizer, skewer each one on a toothpick. Serve with Sweet Red Pepper Chile Sauce for dipping.

Jalapeños Stuffed with Peanut Butter

Lucy Delgado, who was well known in the 1960s as a traditionalist New Mexican cook, taught my father to stuff peanut butter into peppers. "These are the best appetizers I know," she told Dad during one of their recipe swaps. "But if I show you how to make them, you have to promise to try them." Peanut butter–stuffed jalapeños?

"I vowed I would taste them even though they sounded stranger than a five-legged buffalo," Dad commented. When Lucy prepared them, she had a last word of instruction: "Pop the entire pepper in your mouth so you're not left with a mouthful of hot jalapeño and too little peanut butter." Sam'l gamely took the little morsel by the stem and in it went. Miracle! Delicious!

In the 1980s, NBC's *Today Show* came to Denver and Sam'l was a guest. He served Bryant Gumbel our jalapeños stuffed with peanut butter, who devoured all eight Dad had prepared for the show. The TV host couldn't stop eating them! I was amazed he could still talk with his mouth full of pickled jalapeños and gummy peanut butter.

At The Fort, we pickle fresh jalapeños and stir a little mango chutney into the peanut butter. The hand-pickled chiles are far better than canned ones, but if you don't have time to pickle your own, buy Faro brand jalapeños from Mexico.

SERVES 6–8

Ingredients

1 pound Fort-Style Pickled Jalapeños (recipe follows) or 1 (12-ounce) can pickled jalapeños

¾ cup peanut butter (smooth or chunky)

2 tablespoons mango chutney

Directions

1. Slice the pickled jalapeños in half lengthwise not quite all the way through, leaving the two halves attached at the stem end. Using a knife or spoon, remove and discard the seeds and ribs. (After handling hot chiles, be sure to wash your hands thoroughly before touching your eyes or face.)

2. In a small mixing bowl, combine peanut butter and chutney. Stuff the chiles with the peanut butter mixture and press the halves back together. Arrange stuffed jalapeños on a platter and serve. Advise guests to put the whole chile (except the stem) in their mouths before chewing, to get 70 percent peanut butter and 30 percent jalapeño. A nibbler squeezes out the peanut butter, changing the percentages and making the pepper very spicy indeed.

Fort-Style Pickled Jalapeños

Ingredients

1 pound small to medium-size fresh jalapeños

3½ cups cider vinegar

1¾ cups water

½ cup sugar

2½ teaspoons salt

2½ teaspoons sesame oil

1 teaspoon pickling spice

¾ cup coarsely chopped yellow onion

¾ cup coarsely chopped carrot

3 whole cloves garlic, peeled

Directions

1. Rinse the jalapeños and trim off woody ends from the stems.

2. In a 4- to 6-quart stainless steel or enamel pot, combine vinegar, water, sugar, salt, sesame oil, and pickling spice. Add jalapeños, onion, carrot, and garlic. Cover and bring to a simmer over high heat, stirring occasionally. Reduce the heat to low and simmer for 5 minutes. Remove pot from heat.

3. While they are still hot, transfer jalapeños and pickling juice to a sterilized 2- to 3-quart canning jar or other glass container. Cover tightly with lid or plastic wrap and refrigerate for at least 1 week before using.

Oysters and Green Chile

One of the joys of my culinary life is combining foods I really like, and so when I discovered how beautifully oysters and green chile taste together, I was excited. Mild green chile only enhances the flavor of the shellfish.

SERVES 4

Ingredients

2 tablespoons unsalted butter or vegetable oil

3 tablespoons all-purpose flour

¾ cup chicken broth

1 cup chopped green chile

24 freshly shucked oysters in their liquor (see Note)

½ teaspoon salt

¼ teaspoon freshly ground pepper

¼ teaspoon leaf oregano

4 pieces white toast

4 sprigs cilantro or Italian parsley, for garnish

½ red bell pepper, chopped, for garnish

Directions

1. In a sauté pan, melt the butter, then add the flour and stir until it is absorbed. Cook for 1 minute over medium heat until smooth and bubbling.

2. Add the chicken broth and stir until it thickens a little. Add the green chile and heat until boiling. Add the oysters, salt, pepper, and oregano, and turn the heat to low and simmer for 3 to 4 minutes, until the oysters are plump and barely cooked.

3. Serve over toast garnished with a sprig of cilantro or parsley, and red pepper.

Note: If you want a creamier dish, substitute ¼ cup of heavy cream for ¼ cup of the broth. If you cannot find fresh oysters, substitute 2 cups of jarred oysters. Canned oysters are not nearly as good and would be a last resort.

Spirits and Libations

THE FORT'S FAMOUS MOUNTAIN MAN TOAST

This toast was a favorite of my father's, and I have carried on the tradition he started by encouraging its recitation at every conceivable opportunity. On just about any evening at The Fort, you will hear it, getting louder as the toast progresses and those gathered around the table get more into it.

The toast was written in 1988 when Dr. Peter Olch, his wife (Mary), my dad, and my stepmother (Carrie) were invited to Bent's Fort to give lectures. Dad later wrote: *Peter gave his famous speech on "Bleeding, Purging, and Puking," or medicine on the western frontier. I gave a talk on the culinary delicacies of the mountain man [dried buffalo lung with congealed blood pudding among them]. And then, after a long and hot day, we retired to a Mexican restaurant for dinner. All four of us were writers with a good command of early 19th-century words and phrases. It was only a matter of adding a very large pitcher of margaritas before the Mountain Man Toast was born. Since, it has traveled the world over, been printed and reprinted, and has gained a life of its own.*

The toast teaches history in such an entertaining way—and our guests are rewarded with a free drink if they memorize the words and hand gestures—that it is something of a ritual at our restaurant. It's best said with a large group. My dad's good friend Julia Child loved it so much, she said it while wearing a ceremonial headdress!

Here is the toast, with gestures in parentheses and translations following:

> Here's to the child's what's come afore (glass in right hand, held at shoulder)
> And here's to the pilgrims, what's come arter (glass in right hand, arm extended)
> May yer trails be free of griz (left hand over glass, making clawing motion with fingers)
> Yer packs filled with plews (left and right arms extended, making a circle)
> And fat buffler in yer pot! (glass extended, left hand rubbing/pointing at your belly)
> WAUGH! (raise the hand with glass)

TRANSLATIONS:

Child: What the mountain men called one another

Pilgrim: Lightly derisive term used by mountain men for the "sod-busting" covered wagon migrants traveling west

Arter: After

Griz: Grizzly bear, a major cause of death for mountain men

Plews: Large beaver pelts, originating from the French word "plus" (pronounced PLU). Extra-large pelts were marked with a plus sign and were deemed "plews" by the Americans.

Fat buffler in yer pot: Fat, tasty buffalo in your belly

Waugh: Historic mountain man exclamation, meaning "cheers" or "right on"

Bent's Fort Hailstorm Julep

Since the day my father and mother opened The Fort in 1963, this has been a signature cocktail. My dad explains its origins: Back in the 1830s at Bent's Fort in southeastern Colorado, the favorite hot weather drink, especially on the Fourth of July, was the hailstorm. Enjoyed by trappers, voyageurs, Mexicans, and Native Americans alike, it is the earliest known mixed drink in Colorado and was described in a number of journals of the early West. It was originally made with either Monongahela whiskey from Pittsburgh or a wheat whiskey from Taos, 300 miles south of Old Bent's Fort. At The Fort we use a variety of whiskeys or cognac for this bestselling drink.

SERVES 1

Ingredients

3 ounces bourbon, Scotch, or cognac

2 teaspoons confectioners' sugar

2 sprigs fresh mint

Crushed ice to fill a wide-mouth pint Mason jar or julep cup

Directions

Put the alcohol, sugar, and mint in the jar and fill with ice. Secure the lid and shake vigorously 50 times. (If using a julep cup, muddle it with a silver spoon, crushing the mint against the ice and the walls of the jar.) I like to do a little chant to the god of mint during the shaking. The ice will bruise the mint so that it releases its flavor, and the ice will melt a little and dilute the drink. Remove the lid and drink from the jar.

Shrub

The shrub was also drunk at Bent's Fort in the 1830s and 40s. Today, many day trappers and traders still make it for the holidays, and it is prized as a Christmas drink. Essentially, it's dark rum with sugar and citrus juices. Over the decades, all types of fruits, including cherries, were added to the rum to further make its name authentic. This is a very old recipe.

SERVES 4-6

Ingredients

2 pounds sugar

1 quart water

2 cups fresh orange juice

Juice and grated zest of 2-3 lemons

2 quarts dark rum

Directions

1. In a large pot, mix the sugar with the water and bring to a boil over high heat. Reduce the heat to medium low and cook for about 5 minutes or until the syrup is clear. Set aside to cool.

2. In a large jar or jug, mix the orange juice with the juice and zest of 2 lemons. Add the rum and syrup, stir, taste, and add more lemon juice and zest if needed.

3. Cover the jar or jug and let the punch stand for 3 days. Strain and serve.

Real Georgia Mint Julep

My mother, Bay, was from an old Georgia family that claimed Sir Francis Marion as an ancestor. Marion, known as the Swamp Fox, helped the patriots win the Revolutionary War. Bay's heritage gave her rights to creating a genuine Georgia mint julep. My dad captured the rich history of the drink: *In the pre–Civil War South, mint juleps identified a distinct way of life. Business was done on the veranda with a julep or two. Courting, also on the veranda, involved juleps. Thomas Jefferson designed a special julep cup that is still made today. There are numerous rules for making juleps, from how fine to crush the ice and how much sugar to add to how big the silver goblet should be, if a cup should be used instead, and how many mint leaves to add. Further refinements address whether the mint should be spearmint or peppermint, and whether spirits other than cognac or bourbon can be added. Every southerner had his favorite recipe, but this version, served in Mason jars in a tradition begun at the Kentucky horse races, is so good that you'll feel like a hog in hickory nuts. The perfume of the peach makes it especially wonderful.*

SERVES 1

Ingredients

1 teaspoon cold water

1 teaspoon confectioners' sugar

12 sprigs fresh mint leaves

3 ounces cognac

3 ounces peach brandy or whiskey

Crushed ice to fill a wide-mouthed pint Mason jar or julep cup

Directions

Place the water in the jar. Add the sugar and dissolve it. Add the mint, cognac, and peach spirits and fill the jar with ice. Stir with a spoon but do not crush the mint.

TOMAHAWK THE CHAMPAGNE

At The Fort, we "tomahawk" a champagne bottle instead of sabering it as they do in France. We slice a tomahawk down the neck of the bottle and then flick it across the neck. The neck is the weakest point of the bottle and the bottle is pressurized, so the top of the bottle pops off and the champagne spouts from it for each guest to catch in a glass. Be sure to wrap the bottle in a cloth before tomahawking it, because a weak spot other than the neck could crack in your hands. This is rare, but an ounce of prevention is worth a pound of cure.

My dad taught his pal Julia Child how to tomahawk a bottle of champagne, and later that week she taught Jay Leno how to do so when she was a guest on *The Tonight Show.* She gave my dad all the credit, which turned out to be something of a backhanded compliment, as the bottle Julia used was weak and broke all over the set! Although she grabbed a second bottle and tomahawked it perfectly, NBC decided to use the broken bottle take to promote the show.

Jim Bridger

To explain the origin of this drink, I will let my dad do the talking: *We created this drink in 1964 and named it for the great frontiersman Jim Bridger. He was a fur trapper who made a name for himself in the Wind River area of Wyoming as well as other parts of the West. As far as we know, he never came as far south as Bent's Fort, but Alfred Jacob Miller pained Ol' Gabe Bridger (his real name was Gabriel) on horseback in Wyoming wearing a British armored breastplate, a gift from the western-sojourning Scottish lord Sir William Drummond Stewart. One hundred and fifty years later, a descendant of Bridger visited us and enjoyed the drink. She disclosed that Jim had been a teetotaler and would not have added the rum!*

SERVES 1

Ingredients

1 ounce apple juice concentrate

1 ounce fresh orange juice

1 ounce sweet and sour syrup

1 ounce lime juice

½ ounce grenadine

Dash of orgeat syrup or Falernum (almond syrup)

3 ounces Jamaican gold rum

Crushed ice to almost fill a wide-mouth pint Mason jar

Orange slice and maraschino cherry, for garnish

Directions

Stir all ingredients, except the garnish, in the jar. Top with the orange slice and maraschino cherry.

Bear's Blood

When my parents first started serving this drink at The Fort in 1963, they served it in custom-made yellow ceramic bowls with bright red interiors and brown bear handles on either side. Our customers loved them, of course, but we quickly discovered how impractical they were because they could not go through our industrial-size dishwashers without breaking or dulling. We continued to serve Bear's Blood cocktails in the bowls until 1967, offering the bowls for sale to everyone who ordered the drink. When they all were sold—and it didn't take long!—we served the drink in a more conventional glass. Just a few years ago, I got a letter from someone in Rhode Island who had bought one of these old bowls at an antique store and, noting The Fort's name on the bottom of it, contacted me and included a picture. Happily, Bear's Blood bowls live on!

SERVES 1

Ingredients

3 ounces orange juice

3 ounces light rum

½ ounce grenadine

Juice of ½ lime

Dash of orange flower water

Dash of sweet and sour syrup

Crushed ice to half fill a wide-mouth pint Mason jar

Carbonated water, to top

Mint leaf, for garnish

Directions

Stir all ingredients, except the carbonated water and mint leaf, in the Mason jar. Top with carbonated water and a mint leaf.

SISSY BEAR, IN SAM ARNOLD'S WORDS

How do you teach a bear to drink from a bottle? You take a bottle of the bear's favorite drink—root beer or Kool-Aid, in Sissy's case— hammer a nail through the bottle cap in three places to makes small holes, and then give the bottle to the bear. She'll worry it and worry it, first licking the cap, and when she realizes where the sweet bubbly liquid is coming from, she'll suck at the cap. Soon you can give her an open bottle, and she'll hold it up and guzzle the sweet stuff down. It was a great fun to take Sissy into the barroom. When Hermann, the bartender, filled up a bottle with fountain cola, Sissy would belly up to the bar, standing up like a man, and swill it down just like anyone else. Some bar patrons were sure they had reached their drinking limit when Sissy showed up.

The Last Roundup

This cocktail is close to lethal, so on The Fort menu we warn guests that no one can order more than two, unless they arrived and are leaving on horseback. And even in that case, the horse has to know its way home!

SERVES 1

Ingredients

1 ounce Demerara rum

1 ounce white rum

1 ounce Puerto Rican gold rum

1 ounce dark rum (Mount Gay preferred)

4 ounces orange juice

3 ounces sweet and sour syrup

1 ounce Falernum (almond syrup)

½ ounce grenadine

1 cup of crushed ice to fill a wide-mouth pint Mason jar

Carbonated water, to top

Orange slice and maraschino cherry, for garnish

Directions

Stir all liquid ingredients, except the soda water with ice, in the Mason jar. Top with carbonated water and garnish with an orange slice and a cherry.

1732 Philadelphia Fish House Punch

My dad first tasted this punch in his home state of Pennsylvania when he attended friends' weddings and it was the drink of the day. Without a doubt it packs a punch, and while the citrusy drink slides down very easily, it's good to remember that a little goes a long way. We were both excited when, in 1994, we came across a recipe for the punch in Jerry Thomas *Bar-Tenders Guide,* which was published in 1887. Always on the lookout for historic recipes, we immediately added this to our repertoire.

This may well be the oldest punch to be served in America. According to author N. E. Beveridge, who wrote *Cups of Valor* in 1968, it is thought to have originated in the 1600s in London as a farmers' club punch, after which it traveled to the New World and was served at the renowned Fish House Tavern in Schuylkill, Pennsylvania, near Philadelphia. It is also sometimes called Decatur Punch.

MAKES ABOUT 2 QUARTS

Ingredients

1½ pints sweet and sour syrup

¾ pound sugar

½ pint cognac

¼ pint peach brandy

¼ pint Jamaican dark rum

1 pint cold water

Directions

Combine all the ingredients with ice and serve. It tastes so smooth that some guests may not be aware of its power. If you serve it from an unattended punch bowl, post a warning sign.

Original Santa Fe 1848 Gin Cocktail

My father wrote a few sentences about this cocktail. I think his words say it all: At the United States Hotel on San Francisco Street in Santa Fe, New Mexico, travelers in 1848 found that their host was a New Englander who went by the name of Long Eben (short for Ebenezer). He served a concoction called a Gin Cocktail. This slightly sweet but powerful gin drink is a dandy!

SERVES 1

Ingredients

3 ounces gin

Dash of Peychaud's bitters

2 dashes of maraschino liqueur

2 dashes of dry vermouth

2 small cubes of ice

Small lemon slice, for garnish

Directions

Stir all liquid ingredients together with the ice, strain, and serve garnished with a lemon slice.

Hot Buttered Rum

In the words of my dad, nothing beats hot buttered rum on a blustery, cold day: *In Colonial America, rum was plentiful due to trade with the West Indies. Newly made rum was often shipped from Jamaica and other British colonial islands to the London docks, where it rested to age. Some of it, though, was shipped to America, where it was often drunk raw, with just a bit of sugar and water to ease its way down. Even today, nothing in the world tastes better when you've been out on a cold, snowy day than a real hot buttered rum. I like the taste of heavier Mount Gay or Demerara rum in this drink, though not a really dark one, like Myers.*

SERVES 1

Ingredients

6 ounces water

1 rounded teaspoon Hot Buttered Rum Batter (recipe follows)

2 ounces dark rum

Cinnamon stick

Pat of butter

Directions

Bring a bar mug of water to a boil in the microwave. Stir in the batter and the rum. Garnish with a cinnamon stick and top with the butter.

Hot Buttered Rum Batter

MAKES ENOUGH FOR ABOUT 30 DRINKS

Ingredients

16 tablespoons (2 sticks) butter, softened

1 cup dark brown sugar

1 teaspoon ground cinnamon

¼ teaspoon grated nutmeg

Directions

Whip all the ingredients together and store, covered, in the refrigerator.

Yard of Flannel

While this holiday libation may be an acquired taste, once you acquire it you will be in love. It marries the hoppy taste of beer with the warmth of rum-based eggnog and, as my mother used to say, will "warm the cockles of your heart" on a snowy evening. When Dad researched the cocktail, here is what he discovered: *A fine colonial winter specialty in taverns, this hot ale drink takes its name from its lovely soft texture. The Yard of Flannel is a wonderful holiday drink that used to be a favorite among the coachmen, outriders, and waggoneers. Coming out of the tavern, bartenders would hand up a yard-long glass of this to freezing coach drivers perched high above. The recipe sounds far more complicated than it is and is worth the effort in the resulting warmth of body and soul.*

SERVES 4

Ingredients

1 quart good ale

4 large eggs

4 tablespoons sugar

1 teaspoon powdered ginger

½ cup Jamaican dark rum

Grated nutmeg, for sprinkling

Directions

1. Heat the ale in a saucepan.

2. Beat the eggs with the sugar in a blender. Add the ginger, then the rum, and blend well.

3. When the ale is almost boiling, slowly combine the two mixtures, pouring the hot ale a bit at a time into the egg mixture and blending well to prevent curdling. Blend the mixture until it is silky or as soft as flannel. Serve in a large glass sprinkled with nutmeg.

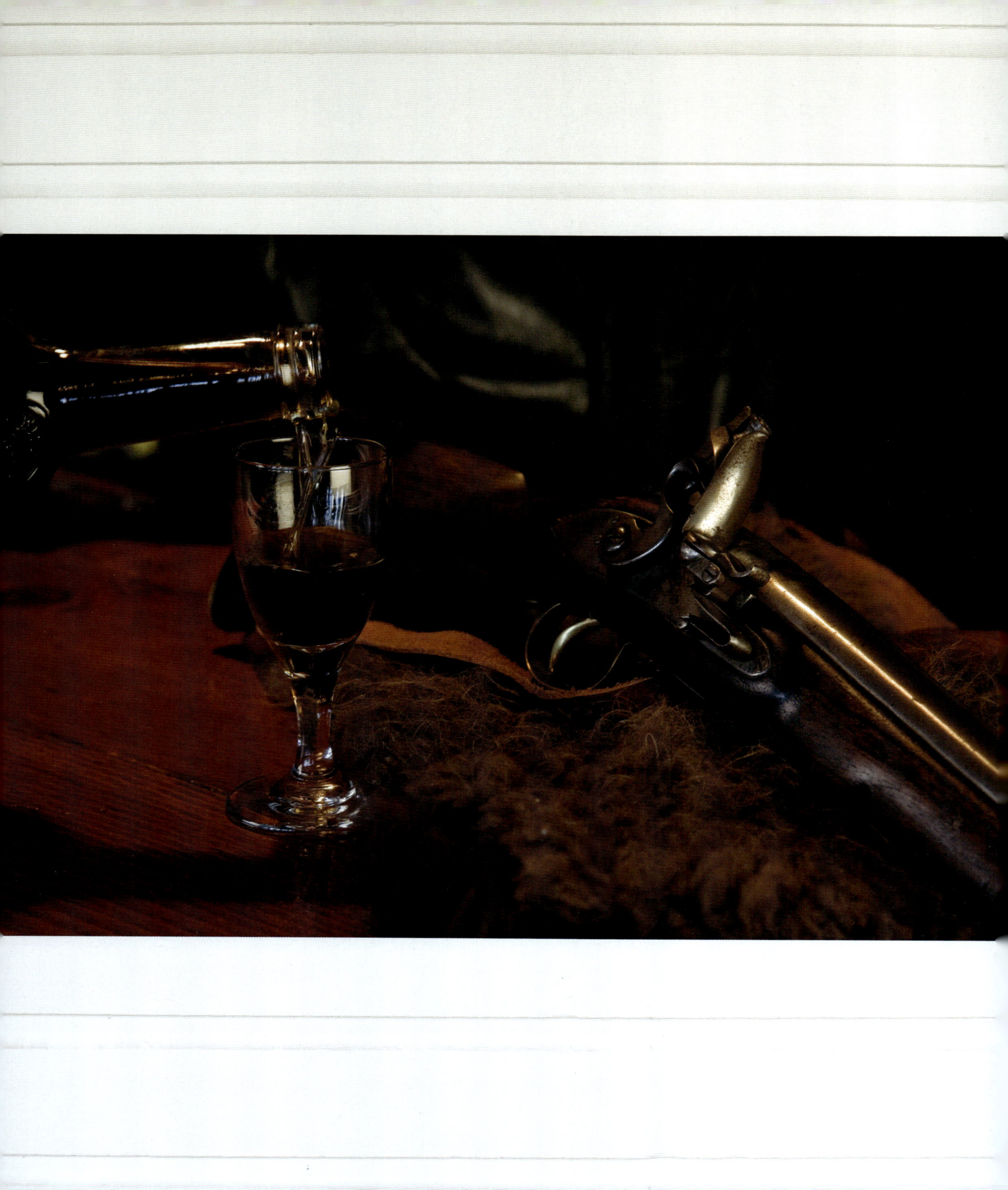

Trader's Whisky

During the temperance movement of the early 19th century, there was a lot of underground contraband liquor sold across our young country. If you cut the liquor with water and other flavorings, handsome profits were to be made. My dad explained it best: *The alcohol that came west, despite federal efforts to limit or eliminate it, was plentiful. It was referred to by many names, among them "great father's milk," "Taos lightning," "belly wash," and "whistle belly vengeance." Traders often watered it down to as little as 3 percent alcohol to extend its profitability. Many strange additives were used to give an interesting taste: red chile, tobacco, or even a liberal pinch of black gunpowder (sulfur, charcoal, and saltpeter). Some said the sulfur was good for a spring tonic, the charcoal kept teeth bright. When ordinary whiskey was later made available to the Indians, they rejected it because it didn't have the good, old-fashioned flavor they were used to. Having read about this concoction in early trappers' journals, I tried it and found it surprisingly good. We began serving it in 1964, and it has remained on the menu ever since. Modern consumers find it both tasty and smooth and many prefer it to regular raw whiskey.*

MAKES 36 SHOTS

Ingredients

1 cup water

2 tablespoons cut tobacco (Virginia Burley preferred)

4 small dried red peppers (piquines)

1 liter Old Crow or similar bourbon whiskey

½ teaspoon black gunpowder (see Note)

Directions

Make a tea by boiling the water, tobacco, and red peppers together for 5 minutes. Strain and add the tea to the whiskey, little by little, to taste. Then add the gunpowder. It should have a gentle nip from the peppers and an herbal taste from the tobacco. The small amount of saltpeter in the black powder will have no effect. Damn!

Note: Do not use modern high-speed powder; it is poisonous!

Prickly Pear Margarita

On summer evenings, our guests like to sit on our patio, enjoying the cool air of the foothills as they gaze down on the city lights of Denver or watch a dramatic sunset. We play classical music—or Erik Many Winds, our Blackfeet musician, plays an Indian flute—and many people sip one of these margaritas, either on ice or frozen. Shinin' times for all!

SERVES 1

Ingredients

2 ounces white tequila (Herradura preferred)

Juice of ½ large lime

1 teaspoon confectioners' sugar

1½ ounces triple sec

1½ ounces prickly pear syrup

½ cup cracked ice

Salt, to rim glass

Slice of lime, for garnish

Directions

Shake all the ingredients except the salt and lime slice in a mixing glass. Strain and serve straight up in a salt-rimmed glass garnished with a slice of lime.

Old-Fashioned Santa Fe Margarita

This recipe is made with the simplest and best ingredients—including only fresh lime juice. The result is one of the best margaritas you'll ever drink.

SERVES 4

Ingredients

Lime wedge and salt, to rim glass

6 ounces tequila (Herradura preferred)

2 ounces premium triple sec

4 ounces lime juice

Directions

Rub the rim of a cocktail glass with lime juice, and dip in salt. Shake all liquid ingredients with ice, strain into the glass, and serve.

PILOT'S COCKTAIL, IN SAM ARNOLD'S WORDS

Since airplane pilots may not drink alcohol for many hours before flying, we developed the Pilot's Cocktail, which is close to an alcoholic drink in taste but without the alcohol. We simply fill a wide-mouth Mason jar with ice and our favorite mineral water, and then add a good squirt or two of Peychaud's bitters. The tiny amount of alcohol in the bitters is insignificant, yet the bitters' flavor provides a wonderfully refreshing drink that's not sweetened with sugar. It's excellent for diabetics, calorie counters, and restaurant owners.

Fort Coffee

Be careful when you order a Fort Coffee. Yes, it's truly delicious, but it's punched with alcohol. Some of our guests have this instead of dessert.

SERVES 1

Ingredients

¾ ounce Bailey's Irish Cream

½ ounce Frangelico (hazelnut liqueur)

6 ounces hot, freshly brewed coffee

Freshly whipped cream, for topping

Directions

Stir the Bailey's and Frangelico together. Pour into the hot coffee, stir once or twice, and serve with whipped cream on top.

Bear Hunter's Tea

When Chris Seres, who has worked at The Fort for more than 30 years, noticed that I had a heavy cold during one of our weekly managers' meetings, he suggested I have a Bear Hunter's Tea. The hot toddy, made with tea and honey liqueur, cured what ailed me!

SERVES 1

Ingredients

6 ounces of water

1 bag orange pekoe or other black tea

2 tablespoons honey liqueur (Bärenjäger preferred)

Lemon slice, for garnish

Directions

Bring the water to a boil. Pour 6 ounces of the water into an 8-ounce cup, with the tea bag inside the cup. Steep the tea in the water for 2 to 3 minutes. Remove the tea bag and stir the honey liqueur into the tea. Garnish with a lemon slice.

ST. VRAIN'S MULE

In the 19th century, just about every kitchen had dried ginger on hand to flavor meat, fowl, sauces, and desserts of all kinds. Gingerbread and gingersnaps were favorite desserts, just as they are today. Ginger beer and ginger brandy were also popular, and most bars served them. The Wayside Inn in East Sudbury, Massachusetts, was known for serving a libation called the Ooo-Ahh!, a mixture of ginger brandy and white rum. Farther west, a drink called St. Vrain's Mule was equally beloved. A mixture of ginger beer and ginger brandy poured into an iced cup or stein, the drink was named in honor of Ceran St. Vrain, who was known for riding a crazy mule. St. Vrain was a partner of the Bent brothers at Bent's Fort, and so we couldn't imagine not including this drink on our menu—and in the book!

Salty Dog with Saddle Leather

We put this cocktail on our menu in 1963 when we opened, and it's been popular ever since. The "saddle leather" is a stick of buffalo or beef jerky garnishing each glass.

SERVES 1

Ingredients

5 ounces grapefruit juice

1½ ounces gin

¼ teaspoon salt

Ice cubes to fill highball glass

Buffalo or beef jerky stick, for garnish

Directions

Pour juice, gin, and salt over ice in the highball glass. Stir well and garnish with a jerky stick.

Vodka may be substituted for gin, if preferred.

1809 Stone Fence

My father wrote about this potent cocktail. However, we still don't know where the name comes from! *In early 19th-century America, drunkenness was rife. Congress passed many laws trying to limit the manufacture and sale of spirits. Rum and whiskey were two major offenders, but the biggest problem was applejack, which nearly everybody could make. Apple cider, once fermented, can be frozen and the alcohol poured off; you don't even need a still. One food historian suggested that the famed Johnny Appleseed, who traveled the countryside planting apple trees, might well have been the publicity man for the distillers' league. Temperance groups literally decimated the apple orchards of early America in an effort to slow alcohol consumption. Fortunately, they didn't succeed in wiping them out. This drink, from Jerry Thomas Bar-Tenders Guide, published in 1887, is a Fort favorite.*

SERVES 1

Ingredients

2 ounces bourbon or rye whiskey

2–3 small cubes of ice

3½ ounces of apple cider

Directions

Combine the bourbon and ice in a 6-ounce bar glass and fill with sweet cider.

Strawberry Sangaree

Fruit sangarees were popular in the days of Bent's Fort. Fruit syrups were combined with red wine and ice for a cool, refreshing drink. Made the same way today at The Fort, they're in high demand during the hot summer months.

SERVES 1

Ingredients

6 ounces red wine

½ cup frozen strawberries in syrup

⅓ cup cracked ice

Directions

Mix all ingredients in a blender and serve in a tall glass.

Virgin Strawberry Sangaree

This is the nonalcoholic version of the sangaree.

SERVES 1

Ingredients

⅔ cup frozen strawberries in syrup

2 ounces sweet and sour syrup

4 ounces sparkling water

Directions

Mix all ingredients in a blender and serve in a tall glass. Nonalcoholic red wine may be substituted for the sparkling water, if preferred.

Colanche Cooler

This refreshing nonalcoholic drink originated in Mexico and is nothing more exotic than fresh fruit juices with a splash of prickly pear syrup. Delicious!

SERVES 8

Ingredients

1 cup prickly pear syrup

1 cup orange juice (freshly squeezed if possible)

1 cup cranberry juice

½ cup fresh lime juice

½ cup fresh lemon juice

Sparkling water, for topping

Lime wedges, for garnish

Directions

Pour the syrup, orange juice, cranberry juice, lime juice, and lemon juice into a half-gallon container. Add enough water to fill the container and stir well. Pour the liquid into tall glasses, filling each about three-quarters full, with or without ice. Top off with sparkling water and garnish with a lime wedge.

Rudesheimer Coffee (Rudesheimer Kaffee)

The company that makes Asbach Uralt brandy suggested to my father in the 1980s that if we carried this popular German coffee spiked with their liqueur, they would give us special coffee mugs to go with the drink! Sold! We have had these special mugs filled with delicious coffee ever since.

SERVES 1

Ingredients

2 sugar cubes

1½ ounces Asbach Uralt

½ cup hot, freshly brewed coffee

Freshly whipped cream, for topping

Chocolate shavings, for topping

Directions

Place the sugar cubes in a mug. Pour the brandy and hot coffee over the sugar. Top with whipped cream and shaved chocolate.

Pomegranate Martini

Pomegranate juice is good for the heart and is beloved in Morocco and now in this country. Our bartender decided we needed a pomegranate martini to heal any broken heart!

SERVES 1

Ingredients

1 ounce vodka (Absolute preferred)

2 ounces Pama liqueur

Splash of cranberry juice

¾ cup ice cubes

Lemon twist, for garnish

Directions

Combine the vodka, Pama, cranberry juice, and ice in a prechilled cocktail shaker. Shake and serve in a chilled martini glass. Garnish with a twist of lemon.

White Ginger Sangria

This delicious and refreshing cocktail is one of The Fort's most popular summer drinks on our patio. After one, you'll say "Ole!" and then order another. A great drink for parties!

SERVES 1

Ingredients

1 slice lime

1 slice lemon

1 wedge orange

6–8 ice cubes

2 tablespoons fresh or frozen huckleberries

1 tablespoon frozen apple juice concentrate

1½ tablespoons ginger liqueur (Domaine de Canton preferred)

4 ounces white wine (preferably Frisk Prickly Riesling)

Directions

In a Mason jar, muddle lime, lemon, and orange. Add ice. In a measuring cup, stir together huckleberries, apple juice concentrate, ginger liqueur, and white wine. Pour over the ice and serve with the jar lid on.

WINES AND BEERS AT THE FORT

The Fort served Robert Mondavi wines when he first opened his Napa Valley vineyard in 1965. My dad and the Mondavis were good friends, and I believe they taught each other a lot about their respective spheres of interest. Dad wanted The Fort to have one of the top wine lists in Colorado and set out to achieve it. He knew a lot of good French wines from Pauillac and Medoc, as well as French Champagne, had been traded along the Santa Fe Trail, and he stocked our cellars with similar vintages. Additionally, we supported wines made in Colorado and New Mexico. New Mexico, believe it or not, became a serious wine region as early as the mid-1800s.

Nowadays, my husband, Jeremy, and I travel to Napa Valley and stay with Jack and Dolores Cakebread of Cakebread Cellars. While in California, we taste a lot of wine with an eye to stocking our cellars. We visit with the Duncans, who own Silver Oak Cellars and are also buffalo ranchers. We see Kate McMurray and Janet Trefethen of Trefethen Family Vineyards, and Joseph Phelps of Joseph Phelps Vineyards. Joseph is a Colorado contractor who was a friend of my father's.

When I joined my father to run The Fort in 1999, we had lost our competitive edge with wine. The industry had become so sophisticated over the years and The Fort had simply not kept up. I was determined to turn this around and quickly. I wanted to earn a *Wine Spectator* award and designation for the restaurant.

We asked our then dining manager, Chris Seres, to expand his position to include managing our wine program. Chris contacted a master sommelier and got to work. They swapped out the mediocre wines for best-selling vintages. They bought little-known but great wines from boutique vineyards and never spent more money than was allocated to our inventory. I was unaware of all Chris was doing, so I was surprised and gratified when he announced that he was applying for *Wine Spectator*'s coveted Award of Excellence. We got it! I was so proud of Chris and am still proud that we have earned this distinction every year for the last eighteen. Chris is currently my assistant general manager, and I am general manager of The Fort. I'm so grateful to Chris for his brilliant mind, hard work, talent, and dedication to our employees and guests.

Today, our staff and customers love the wine program and our exciting, extensive wine list. We like to offer a fair value for our wines. It is our philosophy that if you give good value on good wine with a smaller markup than is standard, your customers will come back and order more wine. This attitude has benefitted us and our customers well for more than 55 years. And let's face it: there is nothing better than a good bottle of cabernet, shiraz, or pinot with a juicy buffalo steak!

The Fort was the first American establishment to serve Carta Blanca beer, imported from Mexico, in 1963, but the most popular beer we had on draft was Coors. At that time, Coors was sold only in Colorado and was a cult beer. Made with Rocky Mountain spring water, it was so good that Coloradoans would smuggle it to friends and families in other states. Coors is brewed in the nearby town of Golden. The Coors family has been coming to The Fort for generations for a good Herman Joseph or golden Coors beer served with our game meat.

Coors hired my dad in 1982 to tour the country as the spokesperson for a historical cookbook the company published. In that book was Pete Coors's great-grandmother's recipe for sauerbraten. During Pete's run for the US Senate, we hosted a dinner for him, serving recipes from his great-grandmother. Pete's uncle, Bill Coors, was in my mother- and father-in-law's wedding, and Bill was also a very close friend of my dad. Coors has always been a great Colorado beer, coming from a wonderful family that contributes so much to our community.

The Fort also serves a large selection of microbrews, as more than 400 breweries call Colorado home!

Chiles and Sauces

CHILES, CHILES, AND MORE CHILES

No one loved chile more than my dad. He started the Colorado chapter of the International Connoisseurs of Green and Red Chile, which in its heyday boasted more than 1,500 members and the motto "Up Your Pod!" As a recognized food historian, Dad wrote about the little vegetable that conquered the world. Here are his words.

In the Middle Ages, Europeans enjoyed a "long pepper," brought to them from India. It was mild but with a discernible undercurrent of heat and cooks loved the zest and life it gave to their dishes. This was the pepper that Christopher Columbus sought when he set sail to find the Spice Islands. When he arrived in the West Indies in 1492, the local people served him foods he'd never encountered—much less imagined. One was a pod pepper, hotter than the long pepper and much more easily stored and transported. The pod pepper had originated on Mexico's Yucatan Peninsula and on his second voyage to the New World, Columbus returned to Spain with its seeds. This chile (or capsicum, as it's also called) spread across the western world to Africa and Asia and today figures prominently in the cuisines of any number of countries around the world. From the remotest Americas through Europe, across India, around Asia, and everywhere in between, chile pods— long, short, thin or fat, red, yellow, green, brown, and purple—have traveled to tantalize man's soul and his palate.

It seems to me that much of chile's popularity worldwide stems from its ability to make otherwise unexciting cuts of meat and many kinds of starches (rice, pasta, potatoes) both flavorful and pepper hot. And of course, one needn't be rich to enjoy it.

It's very versatile, too. The Thai spoon a bit of chicken or pork cooked in a chile-heavy curry sauce over large bowls of rice. The Mexicans add chile-flavored meats to cornmeal tamales. I use it in just about everything. Eating a very hot chile imparts a certain euphoria and for many (including me), it's a virtual addiction.

IS IT SPELLED CHILE OR CHILI?

In my research, I discovered that the ancient *Capsicum* genus, or chile, has been domesticated for more than 7,000 years. Between 5200 and 3400 BC, Native Americans grew chile plants to use for cooking and medicinal reasons. This places chiles among the oldest cultivated crops of the Americas. By 1600, chiles were commercially grown in the United States by the Spanish colonists who settled in the Rio Grande Valley of northern New Mexico.

The word "chile" is derived from the Nahuatl (Aztec) dialect and refers to plants known as capsicum; *aji* or *axi*, also known as chile today, comes from the extinct Arawak dialect of the Caribbean. Chile (ending in *e*) is the authentic Hispanic spelling of the word. English linguists have changed the ending letter to *i*. In fact, the word "chili" refers to the bean-based dish most famous in the state of Texas, not the pepper.

Holly's Ristra Chile Sauce

This is one of my favorites and when I make it, I always leave a few seeds in the pods because I like my chile sauce medium hot. Chiles can surprise you; ones that you expect to be mild are incendiary while the hot-looking ones end up being mild! However, the number of seeds you leave in the pods determines, to some extent, the heat of your finished chile sauce.

MAKES 3 ½–4 CUPS

Ingredients

¼ cup olive oil

¼ cup all-purpose flour

2 tablespoons dried Mexican oregano, divided

3 cups chicken broth

6 dried red New Mexican chile pods

1 cup boiling water

6 cloves garlic, peeled and roughly chopped

½ teaspoon salt, plus more to taste

Directions

1. Place olive oil in a large saucepan over medium heat. Stir in the flour and 1 tablespoon of Mexican oregano. Cook, stirring constantly, for 2 to 3 minutes, until the flour turns golden brown. Slowly whisk in the chicken broth. Continue to cook, stirring, for about 1 minute, until the sauce begins to thicken. Set sauce aside while preparing the chiles.

2. Wearing rubber gloves, rinse the chile pods under lukewarm water. Break off the stems, open the pods, and wash the inside of the chiles. Inside each pod is an oil sack that is connected to the seeds. This membrane and the seeds contain the heat.

3. In a blender, combine the chiles, boiling water, garlic, remaining tablespoon of oregano, and ½ teaspoon salt. Put the lid on and purée.

4. Press the purée through a coarse strainer into the chicken broth–based sauce and stir until well combined. Simmer the sauce, stirring often, for 20 to 30 minutes, adding water to thin it if necessary. Add salt to taste.

Variation: You could use fresh red chile powder in place of the peppers by adding 1 teaspoon of fresh chile powder for every pepper. Do not use commercially made chile powder advertised for use in Texas bean chili. Only use pure ground chile powder.

COLORFUL CHILE RISTRAS

Both ancient and current-day residents of New Mexico and Colorado dried chiles to preserve them for use throughout the winter. More often than not, ripe chiles are gathered in the fall and worked into full, colorful ropes or strands called ristras. These are hung in the kitchen and the fiery little dried chiles are plucked from them, once the cold weather sets in, to flavor stews, rubs, and egg dishes—just about anything and everything.

If you buy a ristra, be sure it isn't shellacked, which means it is meant only for ornamental use. Beautiful chile ristras come in many shapes and sizes, but the most common are the red Anaheim peppers worked into strands ranging from three to six feet long. In New Mexico and Colorado, you find these at roadside vegetable stands in the fall. When you buy a ristra, it's advisable to hang it outside for two or three weeks to air it out and make sure it's completely dry before you bring it inside. Otherwise the chiles could mold.

HOW TO CHAR GREEN
CHILES FOR SAUCE

Start with 12 fresh Anaheim chiles, each about 6 inches long and 2 to 3 inches in diameter. Lay the chiles on a broiler pan and broil for 3 to 5 minutes per side or until you see the skin blistering and charring. Turn the peppers to char all sides. I turn each chile a quarter turn at a time and cook them until the skin bubbles and turns black.

Using tongs, lift the peppers from the broiler pan and transfer the chiles to a gallon plastic bag. Seal the bag and let the chiles stand for about 10 minutes. This is called "sweating" the peppers. Run the peppers under cool water and peel off the blackened skin. The peppers are now ready for chopping. They can be used to make a sauce or draped over any broiled meat. If you don't use them right away, store them in a zipped plastic bag in the refrigerator or freezer. I keep several bags in my freezer all winter and use the chiles as I need them.

Sweet Red Pepper Chile Sauce

My dad liked this sauce with our Buffalo Eggs (page 8) and Rocky Mountain Oysters (page 18),
and it's good over other meats, poultry, and eggs. Surprisingly, it's not made with New Mexico chiles
but from commercial sweet red chile sauce. Easy!

MAKES 1½ CUPS

Ingredients

¾ cup red chile sauce (the
commercial variety, found in
the ketchup aisle)

¾ cup hot mango chutney,
such as Major Grey's

1½ tablespoons yellow
mustard seed

Directions

Mix all the ingredients and chill for at least 6 hours to give the
flavors a chance to mellow and mingle.

Chopped Green Chile Sauce

Everyone seems to have a preference when it comes to chile sauce. For example, my husband, Jeremy, likes green sauce more than red, but lots of folks prefer red chile sauce, in part because of its cheery color. I like both sauces equally and sometimes spoon both red and green on my plate, regardless of what else is on it! At The Fort we make a hot green chile sauce and a mild one, such as this one. It's wonderfully versatile and can be served on the side or spooned into a pocket cut in a thick steak, as we do in the recipe for Gonzales Steak (page 144).

MAKES ABOUT 2 CUPS

Ingredients

10–12 New Mexican green, Anaheim, or California green chiles, roasted and peeled (canned will do, but fresh are best)

½ teaspoon salt, or to taste

2 large cloves garlic, peeled and minced

¼ teaspoon dried Mexican oregano

1–2 teaspoons olive or canola oil

Directions

Slit the chiles to remove the seeds. With a large chef's knife, chop the chiles into a fine dice and mix with the salt, garlic, and oregano. Drizzle with the oil. Serve as a topping or filling for a grilled steak or other grilled meats.

Red Chile Purée

We serve this classic red chile purée at The Fort. My dad does the best job of explaining how our family first discovered it: *Way back in 1949, when I owned a toy store in Santa Fe called La Boutique Fantasque, local artist Will Shuster painted a jack-in-the-box sign for the top of a tall pine pole that had been cut and draw-knife peeled by Taos wood carver and furniture maker Elidio Gonzales. Elidio, a small, thin man with soulful eyes, looked as I imagined Don Quixote might. My wife and I became great admirers of his craftsmanship, and as time passed, his Spanish Colonial furniture was sought by the likes of author Leon Uris and actor John Wayne. Many years later he carved The Fort's doors and our first chairs.*

One Thanksgiving, Elidio invited us to his home. Atop his big carved table were laid a roast turkey, salad, hot flour tortillas, and mashed potatoes that were topped with red chile purée instead of gravy! What a wonderful discovery this turned out to be. In addition to spooning this thick, red sauce over mashed potatoes, we use it with our tamale pie as well as many other dishes. It's also the base for our versatile, smooth, and spicy Red Chile Sauce, which we love with pork chops, steaks, enchiladas, and just about anything else fit to eat!

MAKES ABOUT 2 CUPS

Ingredients

12 dried New Mexican red chiles, rinsed, or ½ cup pure New Mexican ground red chile (Medium Dixon preferred)

1 clove garlic, peeled

½ teaspoon salt, or to taste

½ teaspoon dried Mexican oregano

1–1½ cups hot, boiling water

Directions

1. If using dried chiles, preheat the oven to 300°F. Lay the chiles on a dry baking sheet and bake them for 5 to 7 minutes or just until warmed through and fragrant. As soon as you can handle them, break the stems off the chiles and shake out the seeds.

2. Put the chiles or chile powder, garlic, salt, oregano, and 1 cup of hot, boiling water in a blender and zap into a smooth purée. Be sure to blend long enough to completely purée the garlic. The mixture should be loose and pourable. If necessary, add an additional ½ cup of hot, boiling water.

Red Chile Sauce

Serve this smooth sauce with chicken, quail, pork, beef, buffalo steaks—you name it!

Ingredients

3 ounces canola or avocado oil or any other vegetable oil

4 tablespoons all-purpose flour

1 cup Red Chile Purée (page 59)

½ teaspoon salt (omit if broth is salted)

1 cup chicken broth

Directions

Heat the oil, medium heat, in a sauté pan. Stir in the flour and cook to a golden brown. Add the Red Chile Purée and salt and cook another 30 seconds, stirring constantly. Add the cup of broth little by little, whisking the sauce smooth.

Adobada Marinade for Pork, Chicken, or Beef

This marinade is delicious with almost any meat, poultry, or even fish you want to soak in a full-flavored brew. When you marinate food, use a nonreactive dish—glass or ceramic is best—and marinate meat and poultry for at least 4 hours. When you marinate fish, don't leave it in the marinade for longer than 35 to 45 minutes or it will turn a little mushy.

MAKES ABOUT 1 CUP

Ingredients

½ cup medium red chile caribe (coarsely ground chile)

1 cup chicken broth

½ teaspoon dried Mexican oregano

2 cloves garlic, peeled and minced

½ teaspoon salt

Directions

In a nonreactive (glass) dish large enough to hold the meat or fish, combine the chile, chicken broth, oregano, garlic, and salt. Use the marinade right away or cover and refrigerate for up to 2 days.

Red Chile Honey Glaze

This sweet glaze is as delicious brushed on poultry and fish as on root vegetables. My dad liked it particularly on roasted carrots in the winter; when spring came to the Rockies, Dad would plead with the chef to keep glazed carrots on the menu for a little longer. This is a marvelous example of something that is simple and yet so good.

MAKES ½ CUP

Ingredients

¼ cup raspberry vinegar

¼ cup water

1 tablespoon cornstarch or arrowroot

1 tablespoon Red Chile Honey (recipe follows)

Directions

Mix all ingredients well and store in an airtight container until ready to use.

Red Chile Honey

MAKES ½ CUP

Ingredients

½ cup honey

½ teaspoon ground pure New Mexican red chile powder (Dixon preferred)

Directions

Stir the honey and chile powder until well mixed.

Samoren Sauce

In the 1980s when my son Oren was about 10, he was in the habit of walking over to his grandpa's house on Sunday to cook with GrandSam. Together they came up with this incredible jalapeño sauce, which quickly found its way to The Fort to become one of our favorite sauces for meat with its sweet bite of ginger and mustard. When it came to naming their creation, neither was shy about using both of their names: Sam and Oren, Samoren! This recipe is easily doubled.

MAKES 6 HALF-PINT JARS

Ingredients

2 pounds fresh jalapeño chiles, stems, seeds, and ribs removed

½ pound fresh ginger, peeled

2 cloves garlic, peeled

2 pounds white sugar

4 cups white distilled vinegar

2 cups water

1 tablespoon black mustard seeds

1 tablespoon salt

1 tablespoon pectin

Directions

1. In small batches, purée the jalapeños, ginger, and garlic in a food processor and remove to a large nonreactive (enamel) pot or saucepan.

2. Add the sugar, vinegar, water, mustard seeds, salt, and pectin. Bring to a boil over medium heat. Reduce the heat to low and boil gently, stirring frequently, for 35 to 45 minutes or until the mixture thickens and the sugar reaches the soft-ball stage when dropped in cold water.

3. Wash six half-pint jars, lids, and screw bands in hot soapy water and rinse well. Sterilize the jars by submerging them in boiling water for 10 minutes, then keep them in hot water until ready to fill. Treat the lids and screw bands as directed by the manufacturer. Use tongs to lift the jars out of the hot water and place them, top down, on a clean dish towel to drain.

4. Fill the sterile jars with warm sauce, leaving ¼ inch headspace. Wipe each jar rim with a clean cloth, and close with a treated canning lid and screw band. Place the filled jars on a rack in a canning pot filled with boiling water. The water should cover the jars by at least 1 inch. Bring the water back to a boil, and boil gently for 5 minutes. If you are at an altitude of 1,000 feet or more, add 1 minute to the processing time for each 1,000 feet of altitude.

5. Remove the processed jars to a protected surface and allow to sit undisturbed for 12 hours. Check the seals, remove the screw bands, label the jars, and store the sauce in a cool, dry, dark place. After opening, store in the refrigerator. This sauce makes a marvelous gift!

Chipotle Sauce or Marinade

I love the fact that many sauces can double as a marinade, and this is one of the most versatile. I particularly like this sauce with seafood—it's amazing with shrimp—but it's also terrific with pork and poultry.

MAKES ABOUT ⅔ CUP

Ingredients

½ cup olive oil

1 clove garlic, finely minced

Juice of 1 lemon

3 dashes of chipotle sauce or ½ teaspoon mashed chipotle pepper in adovada sauce

1 teaspoon honey or sugar (optional)

Directions

In a small nonreactive (glass) mixing bowl, combine the olive oil, garlic, lemon juice, chipotle, and honey, if using. Serve as a sauce for shrimp or as a condiment or marinade for seafood, pork, or poultry.

Coffee BBQ Sauce

This sauce makes an excellent accompaniment to many of the beginners in this book, including the empanadas.

Ingredients

1 tablespoon olive oil

½ cup diced yellow onion

1½ teaspoons minced garlic (1 clove)

1 tablespoon coarsely ground coffee

¾ cup hoisin sauce

1 cup ketchup

⅓ cup cider vinegar

⅓ cup brown sugar

¼ cup chicken broth

2 teaspoons Worcestershire sauce

1 teaspoon New Mexican chile powder

½ teaspoon kosher salt

Directions

1. In a large saucepan, over medium heat, warm the oil. Add onion and sauté until translucent, 3 to 4 minutes. Add garlic and cook for 1 to 2 minutes. Stir in coffee and cook 1 minute. Add remaining ingredients and bring sauce to a simmer, stirring occasionally. Remove from heat.

2. Allow sauce to cool, then purée it in a blender. Strain the sauce to remove excess coffee grounds.

3. Store in the refrigerator up to five days. To reheat, place in sauce pan on low heat, until it simmers.

Jack Daniel's BBQ Sauce

Ingredients

1 cup Jack Daniel's or bourbon

1 cup molasses

¾ cup Thai sweet red chili sauce

¾ cup orange juice concentrate

½ cup A.1. steak sauce

¼ cup Worcestershire sauce

½ cup water

Directions

1. In a large, nonreactive saucepan, combine all ingredients. Bring to a boil over medium-high heat, stirring.

2. Reduce heat to low and simmer gently, stirring occasionally, for 20 to 30 minutes, until sauce begins to thicken and is reduced to about 2 cups.

Note: If desired, when preparing Smokehouse Buffalo BBQ Ribs (page 148), add the flavorful reduced rib braising liquid to this sauce (yield will increase to 3 cups).

Chipotle BBQ Sauce

Ingredients

1 tablespoon canola oil

¼ cup diced onion

2 tablespoons minced roasted garlic

1 quart chicken broth

1 (14½-ounce) can fire-roasted diced tomatoes

1½ cups tomato paste

½ cup honey

¼ cup molasses

¼ cup apple cider vinegar

1 (3-ounce can) chipotle peppers in adobo sauce

1 jalapeño chile, seeded

1 tablespoon ground New Mexican red chile (Dixon preferred)

1 tablespoon minced Italian parsley

1½ teaspoons dried Mexican oregano

1 teaspoon ground cumin

1½ teaspoons salt

Juice of ½ lime and ½ orange

Directions

1. In a Dutch oven, over medium-low heat, sweat the onion and garlic in oil until translucent, 3 to 4 minutes. Stir in the remaining ingredients.

2. Bring the sauce to a simmer over medium-high heat. Purée with an emersion blender, then continue to simmer for 20 to 30 minutes over low heat, stirring often, to meld the flavors.

CHILES AND THE FORT

"A day without chile is a day without sunshine!" said Elidio Gonzales, who, in the early days of The Fort, was the brilliant wood carver we employed to craft our chairs and other furniture. He even carved The Fort's front doors, much admired by everyone who passes through them. We agree with Elidio, and at The Fort we cook with what we consider the very best New Mexican chiles, which grow in certain valleys in New Mexico and Pueblo, Colorado.

Like the grapes that are blended into fine wine, chile varietals grown in certain places have distinctive qualities. Hatch, Chimayo, and Dixon are grown near their namesake towns. Most of the chiles we use in our cooking at The Fort come from Hatch and Dixon. I often go through Chimayo to buy the wonderful chipotle chile and green powder sold there, which I use to create extra layers of flavor in sauces, soups, eggs, and rubs for beef and pork.

Our menu is rich with chiles: you will find them on our Gonzales Steak (page 144), in a dipping sauce for Buffalo Empanadas (page 7), and in many other beginners. The techniques presented in this chapter—from selecting to deseeding, roasting, and charring chiles—are easy and add tremendous flavor to many dishes.

Soups

Bowl of the Wife of Kit Carson

In the spring of 1961, two years before opening The Fort, my family and I took a road trip to Mexico in a tiny English Morris Mini Cooper S. When we reached Durango, some 600 miles south of the border, we were told that the best place to eat was the drugstore. The next morning, we watched as a stream of young children came in from the fields to fill family lunch buckets with a special soup sold at the store. It smelled so good, we knew we had to try it.

The bowls we were served held a heady, spicy broth of chicken with nice bites of white meat, nutty garbanzo beans, rice, a touch of oregano, chunks of avocado, and bite-size pieces of soft white cheese. The secret of the amazing flavor, though, was the chipotle chile. The combination of a rich chicken broth and smoky chipotle pepper gave the soup a distinctive bite and delicious smokiness.

Caldo Tlalpeño is the soup's proper name, and when The Fort opened, it was squarely on the

menu. No one could pronounce its name or knew what it meant, and despite its innate deliciousness, the soup did not sell. One day Leona Wood, the septuagenarian who ran our gift shop/trade room on weekends, told us, "I remember my grandmother serving us this dish!" We were thrilled to hear this. Miss Wood happened to be the last granddaughter of frontiersman Kit Carson, and with a little genealogical figuring, we dubbed the soup Bowl of the Wife of Kit Carson. It has been a best-selling signature dish ever since.

SERVES 4–6

Ingredients

2 whole boneless, skinless chicken breasts (about 2 pounds)

4–6 cups chicken broth

¼ teaspoon dried Mexican leaf oregano, crumbled

1 cup cooked rice

1 cup cooked, dried garbanzo beans (chickpeas) or canned garbanzos, rinsed and well drained

1 chipotle chile en adobo (canned), minced

4–6 ounces Monterey Jack or Havarti cheese, diced

GARNISH

1–2 ripe avocados, peeled, pitted, and sliced

4–6 sprigs fresh cilantro (optional)

1 fresh lime, cut into 4–6 wedges

Directions

1. Place the chicken breasts and broth in a large saucepan. Bring to a boil over medium-high heat, skimming off and discarding any foam that rises to the top. Turn off the heat, cover, and allow the chicken to poach gently for 12 minutes.

2. Remove the chicken from the pot and cut into strips about 1½ inches long. Return the chicken strips to the broth and add the oregano, rice, garbanzos, and chipotle.

3. Divide the cheese among 4 to 6 deep soup bowls.

4. Return the soup to a boil, then ladle it into the bowls. Garnish each portion with avocado slices, cilantro (if using), and a wedge of lime. Serve with hot tortillas as an appetizer, or with Duck Quesadillas (page 9) as a main course.

Curried Butternut Squash Soup

Inspired by the familiar squash soups found throughout the Southwest and flavored with East Indian curry—traded at Bent's Fort in the 19th century—this delicious soup appears on our menu with happy regularity as a soup special. It is perfect served on a cold evening with cornbread and a green salad.

SERVES 4-6

Ingredients

1 large butternut squash
(about 3 ½ pounds)

3 tablespoons unsalted
butter or vegetable oil

2 large leeks (white and
yellow part only), rinsed
thoroughly and chopped

4 teaspoons fresh ginger
root, peeled and minced

1 tablespoon curry power
(Madras preferred)

⅛–¼ teaspoon cayenne
pepper, to taste

4–6 cups chicken or
vegetable broth

Salt, to taste

GARNISH
2–3 tablespoons minced
Italian parsley

4–6 tablespoons crisp,
crumbled bacon

4–6 tablespoons mild goat
cheese

3–4 tablespoons hulled
squash seeds (pepitas),
lightly toasted (optional)

Directions

1. With a large, sharp knife, cut squash in half lengthwise. Scrape out the seeds and stringy inner portions.

2. To cook in a conventional oven: Preheat the oven to 350°F. Place the squash halves cut side down in a baking pan and add enough water to come 1 inch up the sides. Cover the pan tightly with aluminum foil and bake for about 1 hour, until squash is tender when pierced with a knife.

3. To cook in a microwave oven: Place squash halves cut side down in a microwave-safe dish with ½ inch of water. Cover the dish with microwave-safe plastic wrap and cook on high for 12 minutes. Allow squash to sit in the microwave without removing plastic for 10 to 15 minutes.

4. When the squash is cool enough to handle, use a large spoon to scoop out the pulp and set it aside. Discard the skin.

5. Place the butter or oil in a heavy-bottomed soup pot over medium-low heat. Add the leeks, ginger, curry, and cayenne and cook, stirring, until leeks are softened but not browned, 5 to 7 minutes. Stir in the squash and 4 cups of broth. Season to taste with salt.

6. Bring to a simmer over medium-high heat. Reduce heat to medium-low and cook, stirring and breaking up the squash with a spoon, for 20 minutes.

7. Carefully transfer the mixture to a food processor or blender and purée until smooth. Return the purée to the pot, and if the soup seems too thick, add additional broth. Taste and add more salt, if needed. Bring the soup to a simmer over medium heat, stirring, until heated through.

8. Ladle the soup into warmed bowls and garnish each serving with parsley, crisp bacon crumbles, and a tablespoon of goat cheese placed in the middle of the bowl. Toasted squash seeds are also a very good garnish for this soup.

Note: Curry powder may discolor wooden and plastic utensils as well as food processor blades.

Holly's Posole

During our Indian Market and Powwow at The Fort, held in early June, we make this dish for the visiting artists. They love it, and I am not surprised they do, as it's my personal favorite. When I need a little comfort in this complicated world, this is what I crave. With each bite, I experience the tastes of the ancient ones as they weave a rich tapestry with those cultures that followed.

I nearly always make this with frozen posole, which is sold with other frozen Mexican food in many supermarkets. If you cannot find it, use dried posole, soaked overnight and then boiled according to the package directions.

SERVES 8–12

Ingredients

2–3 tablespoons olive oil

1 large white or yellow onion, peeled and chopped (about 2 cups)

3 cloves garlic, peeled and crushed

1 pound lean boneless pork shoulder, cubed for stew

1½–2 tablespoons dried Mexican oregano, crumbled, to taste

1 large bay leaf

2 pounds frozen posole, defrosted (see Note)

1 gallon equal parts water, chicken broth, and beef broth (see Note)

½ pound fresh medium to mild green chiles, peeled, seeded, and chopped, or frozen chiles, chopped

Salt, to taste

GARNISH

2 cups grated Monterey Jack cheese

6 serrano chiles, seeded and minced

3 limes, cut into wedges

Directions

1. Place olive oil in a Dutch oven over medium heat. Add onion, garlic, and pork. Cook, stirring occasionally, until the pork is browned and the onions caramelize. This may take up to 15 minutes. Do not stir too often, as you need the onions, pork, and garlic to brown well. This process adds flavor! Add oregano and bay leaf.

2. Stir in posole, 12 cups of broth mixture, and the green chiles. Bring to a boil, then reduce heat to low and simmer, covered with lid, for at least 3 hours, stirring occasionally and adding more liquid as necessary. Taste, and add salt if needed.

3. Ladle the steaming-hot posole into bowls and garnish with grated cheese, minced serrano chiles, and lime wedges. Serve with warm flour tortillas.

Note: When buying frozen posole make sure that the ingredients listed include corn, lime, and salt. For the mixed-broth liquid, I use a concentrated chicken and beef bouillon paste, which I add "to taste" for rich flavor. I do not recommend the Tetra Brik stocks sold at supermarkets, as they don't give enough richness of flavor. If making your own stock, reduce it to a concentrate for the best flavor.

POSOLE AND ITS POSSIBILITIES

Posole (sometimes spelled pozole) is a stew made of hominy, pork, green and/or red chiles, garlic, Mexican spices, and meat broth. Every Southwest Indian and Hispanic family has its own recipe for posole, which is considered comfort food and usually prepared for major feast days, such as Christmas. In New Mexico, more pork is sold for posole during the winter holidays than turkey, ham, roast beef, or goose.

Posole is also the name of the particular corn used in the stew. Nowadays, I rely on frozen posole for most uses, but when I can't find it, I soak dried posole overnight and then boil it according to its package directions.

European settlers in the New World observed the Indians pouring water through the ashes from their fires to make a caustic solution. They boiled dried kernels of corn in this ash water until the hard covering of the kernels loosened and floated to the surface. The skins were discarded, and the remaining soft corn kernel was cooked or dried and ground into meal. The partially cooked kernels are what people in the Southwest and Mexico call posole.

When the Spanish settled here, they brought horses, sheep, pigs, and many foods unfamiliar to the Indians. Over time, the indigenous people adopted the domestic animals and used them as an additional food source, which explains why so many posole recipe include pork or other meats and poultry. Today's recipes commonly include garlic and onions from the Spanish and hominy corn, chiles, and Mexican oregano from Native Americans.

Heirloom Bean Soup

During an excavation at Mesa Verde, the ancient Anasazi ruins in the Four Corners region of Colorado, archeologists discovered small, colorful beans still in pots dating from 1200 AD. When cultivated, the beans sprouted, and now Anasazi beans are sold commercially—literally having been rescued from oblivion. Other ancient beans have been revived as well, such as Zuni Golds and brown tepary beans.

I make this soup in a micaceous clay pot that I bought from Debbie Carrillo after seeing her demonstrate the art of micaceous clay pot cooking at the Tesoro Cultural Center's Spanish market. Debbie is one of the notable artists who visit The Fort during our annual 1840's Rendezvous and Spanish Colonial Market, and while I was amazed by the pot, I was not surprised that she recognized and harnessed its properties. The clay is more than 60 percent shiny mica, a mineral. When the clay is formed into pots, the handles stay cool while the minerals distribute the heat evenly and cook the beans perfectly when set directly over the fire. It's easy to get a sense of the ancient Indians cooking these same beans in a similar pot, smelling the same aromas and anticipating the meal as eagerly as we do today. I love the connection.

You don't have to use a micaceous clay pot for this recipe. A good stainless steel bean pot, or any heavy pot that distributes heat evenly, will work. If your pot is made of cast iron, be sure it has been well seasoned so that the iron does not flavor the soup.

SERVES 4-6

Ingredients

½ cup brown tepary beans (see Note)

½ cup Anasazi beans

½ cup Zuni Gold beans

2 small ham shanks (see Note)

2 tablespoons olive oil

1 large yellow onion, peeled and diced

3 medium celery stalks with leaves, chopped

2 cloves garlic, peeled and minced

1-2 tablespoons mild to medium ground New Mexican red chile, to taste

1 teaspoon ground sage

Salt, to taste

⅓ cup hulled sunflower seeds, toasted

Fresh cilantro or sage leaves

Directions

1. Pick over, rinse, and soak the beans in cold water to cover. Some cooks soak beans overnight, and others cook the dried, rinsed beans right away and simmer them for a much longer time. At high altitudes, you will need to cook the beans for at least an additional hour (step 4).

2. Drain the beans and place them in a heavy-bottomed soup pot along with 7 cups of cold water. Bring to a boil over medium-high heat, then reduce heat to low.

3. Meanwhile, place the olive oil in a large, deep skillet or sauté pan over medium heat. Add onion, celery, and garlic and sauté until the onions are caramelized and the garlic is light golden brown, 3 to 5 minutes.

4. Add the sautéed vegetables, ground chile, and sage to the beans. Simmer until the beans are tender, 2 to 3 hours.

5. Season the soup to taste with salt. Remove the ham shanks. Cut the meat off the bones and return it to the soup.

6. Ladle the hot soup into bowls. Garnish with toasted sunflower seeds and fresh cilantro or sage.

Note: To buy the heirloom beans specified in this recipe, turn to "Where to Find It!" I prefer ham shanks to hocks because shanks have more meat and less fat.

Buffalo Vegetable Soup

There is nothing particularly unusual about this soup, unless you think buffalo is out of the ordinary! For us at The Fort, buffalo is as common as a beautiful sunset over the Rocky Mountains, but for many folks, it's exotic. While you could make this with beef, if you can find buffalo—also called bison—you will be rewarded with lean meat that is low in cholesterol and high in iron. We make this popular and hearty soup with organic vegetables so that it's not only one of the tastiest on the menu, but one of the most healthful, too. It can easily be a main course, served with nothing more than freshly baked Bannock Bread (page 129) or Jalapeño Cornbread (page 127).

SERVES 4–6

Ingredients

1 cup diced zucchini

½ cup diced yellow onion

½ cup diced red bell pepper

2 tablespoons canola oil

2 cups diced leftover buffalo or beef roast

8 cups chicken broth

½ cup shelled edamame, frozen

½ cup corn kernels, fresh or frozen

1 cup roasted tomatoes, fresh or canned

1 tablespoon tomato paste

1 tablespoon minced fresh garlic (2 large cloves)

1 teaspoon dried thyme

Salt and freshly ground pepper, to taste

3–4 tablespoons minced fresh cilantro or Italian parsley

Directions

1. In a large, heavy-bottomed soup pot, over medium-low heat, sweat zucchini, onion, and red pepper in oil for 3 minutes. Add buffalo and cook 5 minutes. Add broth and bring to a boil over medium-high heat, stirring occasionally. Add edamame, corn, roasted tomatoes, tomato paste, garlic, thyme, and salt and pepper.

2. Simmer the soup for 35 to 45 minutes, skimming any foam or fat from the top. Garnish with minced fresh cilantro or parsley and serve.

Simple Shiitake Mushroom Soup

Even before my parents built The Fort, they were intrigued with the foods of the West, and so each fall we hiked into the mountains to forage for mushrooms. When we found fresh morels, chanterelles, and boletus (also known as *cepes* in France and *porcini* in Italy), we photographed them for identification and then stowed them away in anticipation of supper. When it was time to eat, my mother sautéed them in butter in a soup pot set over the campfire. She added chicken stock and cream, plus a little tarragon and chervil, and sometimes deglazed the pot with a splash of dry vermouth. If she had it, she sprinkled a little nutmeg on top. The resulting soup was like a first kiss!

This recipe, designed to be made in a kitchen and not over a campfire, relies on a blender or food processor to purée the soup. I am sure if my mother had had a food processor on the trail, she would have used it!

SERVES 4–6

Ingredients

1 pound fresh shiitake mushrooms or 2–3 ounces dried shiitake

3–4 cups reduced-sodium chicken broth

1 pint (2 cups) heavy cream

2 teaspoons minced fresh tarragon or ½ teaspoon dried tarragon

1 teaspoon minced fresh chervil or ¼ teaspoon dried chervil

Salt and freshly ground pepper, to taste

Fresh tarragon or Italian parsley

Directions

1. Trim off and discard woody or discolored stem ends from fresh mushrooms. Separate stems from caps, then wipe stems and caps with a damp cloth.

2. If you are using dried mushrooms, reconstitute them in hot water to cover and don't use the stems, because they'll be too tough. Save the broth; strain out any dirt and grit by pouring the liquid through a coffee filter. You can substitute this liquid for some of the chicken broth.

3. Place mushrooms and 3 cups of broth in a large saucepan. Boil the mushrooms in broth over medium-high heat for 10 minutes. Allow to cool slightly, then purée in a food processor or blender.

4. Return purée to the saucepan and stir in cream, tarragon, and chervil. If the soup seems thick, add remaining chicken broth. Simmer for 15 to 20 minutes.

5. If you prefer a perfectly smooth soup, pour it through a conical sieve (chinois) to filter out any remaining solids. Ladle hot soup into warmed bowls. Garnish with fresh herb sprigs and serve with hot crusty bread.

Chile con Carne, New Mexican Style

My dad made this recipe when my brother and I were kids, and it's always been a family favorite. Not surprisingly, when Dad opened The Fort in 1963, he put the chile on the menu for special occasions. He wrote: *When I first lived in Santa Fe in 1948, I learned from restaurateur Luis Salazar how to make real New Mexican chili con carne. Mr. Salazar came from a long line of Santa Fe-ans and at his Original Mexican Café on College Street, everything was made from scratch. He boiled the blue kernel corn in huge kettles with slaked lime to make posole and the masa for corn tortillas. He dried ripe red Espanola Valley chiles and then stemmed, cleaned, and cooked them to make red chile con carne, which translated means "chile with meat."*

Mr. Salazar's chile con carne recipe reflects the cuisine of the little villages north of Santa Fe, which is very different from those in southern New Mexico, Texas, and Arizona. It contains no beans, no tomato, no onion, no cumin, and only a slight touch of garlic and Mexican leaf oregano. Twice cooking the pork, first to poach it and then to brown and caramelize it, gives the chile great depth of flavor. The longer you simmer it, the more tender the pork will be and the thicker the chile. Additional cornmeal will thicken it, too.

This dish is easy to digest because it contains no tomatoes, which are acidic and contribute to indigestion. Once you taste it, you may never go back to the tomato-and-kidney-bean-based recipes.

SERVES 4–6

Ingredients

2 pounds bone-in pork shoulder (pork butt), trimmed and cut into fist-size pieces

2 tablespoons vegetable oil or rendered pork or bacon fat

¼ cup cornmeal (blue, yellow, or white)

¼ cup cold water

½ cup Red Chile Purée (page 59)

½ teaspoon dried Mexican leaf oregano

Salt, to taste

Directions

1. For best results, start this recipe a day ahead to give the broth time to cool completely so that it can be thoroughly defatted.

2. Place pork in a heavy-bottomed soup pot and add enough water to cover. Bring water to a boil over high heat, then reduce heat to low, cover, and simmer pork gently for 1½ hours. Remove the meat to a large bowl and place the broth in the refrigerator. When the pork is cool enough to handle, cut the meat away from the bone and dice into ¼-inch cubes. Store in the refrigerator until ready to use.

3. Skim off fat from the top of the chilled pork broth. Bring the defatted broth to a simmer. Heat the oil in a deep skillet until smoking. Dry reserved pork cubes with a paper towel and sear in the oil until thoroughly browned. Add the browned meat to the broth. Add ½ cup of broth to the skillet and stir to loosen and incorporate the browned bits.

4. Stir together the cornmeal and water. Add this mixture to the broth in the skillet, stirring well to thicken. Remove about ½ cup broth from the soup pot and set aside in case the chile needs thinning after it has simmered.

5. Pour the broth-and-cornmeal mixture into the soup pot and add the Red Chile Purée. Adjust the seasonings with oregano and salt. Simmer for 20 to 30 minutes to blend flavors, then serve piping hot.

CUSTOM-MADE FURNITURE AT THE FORT

Antonio Archuleta from Taos, New Mexico, custom-made Spanish Colonial–style furniture for The Fort from the day we opened in 1963. He was also a master builder and brilliant wood carver, and much of our furniture displays his artistry—as does some of the furniture in my own home, I am pleased to say, where a king-size master bed, guest beds, and a beautiful *trastero* (cabinet) with intricate carvings make me smile every day. In my opinion, there was no finer artisan making traditional Spanish Colonial–style pieces than Antonio.

Antonio learned his craft from Elidio Gonzales in the 1950s and in the ensuing years won more awards at the Santa Fe Spanish Colonial Market than anyone could count. He always called my father his "gringo daddy," while I was *mi hermana* ("my sister"), and Jeremy, my husband, was *mi hermano* ("my brother"). Antonio hand-made all the Padre Martinez chairs at the restaurant without nails, instead relying on tongue-and-groove construction.

Sadly, Antonio passed away in 2011. Our current amazing furniture maker is award-winning Spanish Colonial artist Randy Martinez from Santa Fe, New Mexico. We serve more than 350 customers a day, and so over the years, we've had thousands of chairs hand-made for us by either Elidio, Antonio, or Randy. Visitors to The Fort also take note of Antonio's beautiful benches, and cabinets. All are spectacular!

Holly's Root Vegetable Soup

Honestly, when I was trying to lose some weight, I made a basic vegetable soup but quickly discovered I wanted more flavor and substance to fill my belly. To satisfy my hunger, I started using primarily root vegetables and caramelizing the onions and other veggies before adding them to the broth. Now, I make a large pot of this nearly every Sunday and portion it into small plastic containers. I refrigerate two or three and freeze the rest. There's lunch or even supper! Delicious, nutritious, and filling. I confess, this soup has never made it onto the menu at The Fort, but I couldn't write a book without including it. It's that good and tastes even better on the second day—you will never go back to canned soup again. If you're not trying to cut as many calories as possible, serve this with Pumpkin-Walnut Muffins, Quinoa Muffins (page 134), or Bay's Southern Spoon Bread (page 135).

SERVES 4–6

Ingredients

1 small yellow or white onion

1 celery stalk

1 small turnip

1 small rutabaga

1 carrot

1 small sweet potato

10 fingerling potatoes, washed but not peeled and cut in half

1 small fresh fennel (anise) bulb, trimmed and diced

2 cloves garlic, peeled and minced

2–3 teaspoons herbes de Provence

1 bay leaf

2 tablespoons olive oil

6 cups chicken broth or vegetable broth

1 (6-ounce) can tomato paste

1 cup shredded cabbage (optional)

GARNISH

4–6 tablespoons mild goat cheese

2–3 slices bacon, cooked crisp and crumbled

4–6 sprigs Italian parsley

Directions

1. Peel and dice the onion, celery, turnip, rutabaga, carrot, and sweet potato.

2. Place olive oil in a heavy-bottomed soup pot. Add all vegetables and herbs and sauté over medium heat, stirring every 2 to 3 minutes, for 4 to 6 minutes or until the edges of the onion, celery, and fennel begin to caramelize. Continue to cook over low heat, stirring occasionally, until the other vegetables have softened, 15 to 20 minutes. This browning adds flavor!

3. Add broth, tomato paste, and shredded cabbage (if using), and bring to a boil over medium-high heat. Reduce heat to low and simmer, stirring occasionally, for 30 minutes.

4. Ladle soup into bowls and garnish each serving with 1 tablespoon of goat cheese, a sprinkling of crumbled bacon, and a sprig of parsley.

Navajo Zucchini-Jalapeño Soup

Our former chef Juan Zapata, at The Fort was inspired by how the Navajo, or Diné, as they are also called, use chiles, corn, and squash. To highlight Navajo methods, he developed this masa-based soup, which rapidly became extremely popular with our guests. The masa, or blue cornmeal, thickens the soup and the chiles provide enough bite without being too spicy. The toasted pepitas add nuttiness and a wonderful sense of ancient comfort food. Chef Juan told me that in his native Mexico, soups are usually the main course and not just a first course. This soup could easily fill that role served with Quinoa Salad with Fresh Garden Mint (page 90) and Pumpkin-Walnut Muffins (page 132).

SERVES 4–6

Ingredients

1 pound zucchini (2–3 zucchini)

½ pound russet potatoes (1–2 potatoes)

½ cup chopped yellow or white onion

½ cup diced mild green chiles

1 small jalapeño chile, peeled and seeded

¼ cup fresh cilantro leaves

1 teaspoon minced garlic (1 clove)

3 tablespoons minced fresh shallot (1 medium)

6 cups vegetable or chicken broth

1 cup corn niblets, fresh, frozen, or canned

Salt and freshly ground pepper, to taste

⅓ cup masa harina

⅓ cup cold water

½ cup hulled pumpkin seeds (pepitas) or sunflower seeds, lightly toasted

Fresh cilantro sprigs, for garnish

Directions

1. With a vegetable brush, scrub zucchini and potatoes under cold running water. Slice zucchini, and peel and coarsely chop potatoes.

2. Place zucchini, potatoes, onion, mild chiles, jalapeño, cilantro, garlic, and shallot in a heavy-bottomed soup pot. Stir in broth. Bring to a boil over medium-high heat, stirring occasionally. Cover and reduce heat to low. Simmer, stirring occasionally, for about 30 minutes or until zucchini and potatoes are tender when pierced with a knife.

3. Allow mixture to cool slightly, then purée in a food processor or blender. Return puréed soup to the pot and stir in corn. Bring the soup to a boil over medium heat, then reduce to a simmer. Season to taste with salt and pepper.

4. In a large measuring cup, stir together masa harina and water. Gradually whisk the masa mixture into the soup. Simmer, continuing to whisk until masa is incorporated and the soup has thickened. Taste again and adjust seasonings. Ladle hot soup into bowls and garnish with toasted pepitas and cilantro.

Holly's Tarragon Gazpacho

Although the Rocky Mountains that surround The Fort are snow-capped year-round, it gets hot and dry in the mountains in the summertime, and nothing hits the spot more deliciously than this refreshing cold soup. I love to use summer's best tomatoes, cucumbers, and scallions from the farmers' market and fresh herbs from my small garden. Gazpacho is a Spanish soup and seems to fit perfectly into our southwestern lifestyle.

SERVES 4–6

Ingredients

1½ cups peeled, diced, fresh plum tomatoes or 1 (14 ½-ounce) can diced tomatoes

½ cup peeled, chopped cucumber

½ cup chopped scallions (2–3)

2 tablespoons tarragon vinegar

1 large clove garlic, peeled

2 cups spicy Clamato juice (or V8), chilled

3 tablespoons minced fresh tarragon

½ teaspoon hot pepper sauce, if you can't find spicy Clamato or V8

Salt, to taste

GARNISH

½ cup homemade croutons, fried in olive oil

½–¾ cup sour cream

4–6 sprigs fresh basil

1–2 ripe avocados, peeled and sliced (optional)

Directions

1. Place the tomatoes, cucumber, scallions, vinegar, and garlic in a food processor or blender. Pulse on and off until vegetables are chunky. Pour into a large bowl. Stir in vegetable juice, tarragon, and pepper sauce, if using. Salt to taste. Cover, and refrigerate until well chilled.

2. Garnish with croutons, 2 tablespoons of sour cream placed in the center of each bowl, and sprigs of fresh basil. As an alternative, slices of avocado are also a beautiful garnish.

Salads and Dressings

Cherry Tomato, White and Anasazi Bean Salad

This simple salad is a colorful and tangy accompaniment to grilled foods, or delicious for a light lunch with toast and honey. Be sure to marinate the red onions in the vinaigrette for at least 15 minutes.

SERVES 4

Ingredients

⅛ cup olive oil

3 tablespoons red wine vinegar

2 tablespoons fresh lemon juice (Meyer lemons preferred, as they're sweeter)

1 tablespoon good Dijon mustard (Maille preferred)

1 teaspoon kosher salt, or to taste

1 teaspoon pepper, or to taste

¾ cup thinly sliced red onion (½ onion)

1½ teaspoons minced garlic (1 large clove)

2 pints cherry tomatoes, halved

1 (15-ounce) can cannellini beans, or great northern, rinsed and drained

1 cup cooked Anasazi beans (optional), rinsed

⅓ cup chopped fresh Italian parsley or cilantro

½ cup shaved Parmigiano-Reggiano cheese

Directions

1. In a small bowl, whisk together the olive oil, vinegar, lemon juice, mustard, salt, and pepper. Stir in red onion and garlic. Set aside to marinate the onions for at least 15 to 30 minutes at room temperature.

2. Place the cherry tomatoes, beans, and parsley/cilantro in a larger bowl. Pour the marinade over the salad, toss well, and then gently stir in the shaved cheese. Serve at room temperature.

Quinoa Salad with Fresh Garden Mint

This salad is like a Middle Eastern tabbouleh because it relies on tomatoes and fresh garden mint. It is one of The Fort's favorite side dishes, particularly because we use full-flavored, juicy heirloom tomatoes. Our customers love it with The Fort's Herbed Lamb Chops (page 179) in the spring and summer and as a complete protein salad served with our Three Sacred Sisters Tamale Pie (page 208) or any of our soups.

SERVES 4–6

Ingredients

1½ cups (8 ounces) quinoa

1 cucumber, peeled, seeded, and diced

⅓ cup fresh mint leaves, minced

⅓ cup Italian parsley, minced

⅓ cup fresh lemon juice

⅓ cup olive oil

Salt and ground black pepper, to taste

2 ripe tomatoes (preferably heirloom varieties), seeded and diced

Directions

1. In a large fine-mesh strainer, rinse the quinoa under cold running water and drain well. Place the quinoa and 2 ½ cups of water in a large saucepan and bring to a boil over high heat. Reduce the heat to low, cover, and simmer until most of the water has been absorbed, 15 to 20 minutes. When done, the grain appears translucent, and the germ ring will be visible. Drain the cooked quinoa and spread it out in a shallow baking pan to cool.

2. After the quinoa is completely cool, place it in a salad bowl, and add the cucumber, mint, and parsley.

3. In a small mixing bowl, whisk together the lemon juice and oil. Season the dressing to taste with salt and pepper. Drizzle the dressing over the quinoa, add the tomatoes, and toss gently. Taste the salad and adjust the seasonings.

MY DAD DISCOVERED QUINOA IN PERU. HERE'S THE STORY IN HIS OWN WORDS

In the mid-1970s on a trip to Peru, I learned of the grain called quinoa (KEEN-wah). The individual grains are tiny balls and have a texture similar to black lumpfish caviar. Quinoa takes on the flavors of the foods with which it's mixed, but its most significant feature is that it contains more usable protein than any other grain in the world, including amaranth, rice, and spelt. Dr. John McCamant, a former professor at Denver University and one of the country's experts on quinoa, says that it is close to being the perfect food.

Archaeological evidence shows that quinoa was cultivated as early as 5000 BC in the Ayacucho Basin in Peru. It was a staple of the Andean peoples and was held sacred by the Incas, who called it the mother grain.

I was so excited about it that I immediately wanted to begin importing the grain to the United States until I discovered that a man named Stephen Gorad in Boulder, Colorado, was already importing and selling it to specialty grocers. Eventually, he sold his company to a conglomerate in California and today quinoa enjoys sales nationwide. It will never compete with grains such as wheat because it lacks gluten for making yeast bread and because it is difficult to grow, but it's becoming better known all the time.

Quinoa's native environment is near the equator, which means a long growing season high in the Andes at altitudes ranging from 7,000 to 13,000 feet above sea level. This means cool temperatures. After many years of research and experimentation, in the 1980s quinoa was finally cultivated successfully in the Rocky Mountains. Today, White Mountain Farms, high in Colorado's San Luis Valley, grows (in addition to excellent potatoes) several strains of what has been dubbed the super grain of the future. White, tan, and black varieties of quinoa are available, but the original black grain, from which the others have derived, is by far the best. In Peru, it's called coital quinoa, although I haven't been able to find out why.

The preparation of quinoa is easy. The plant grows to about six feet and has a large seed-covered head coated with a natural soap to discourage animals and insects from eating it. This is rinsed off in the commercial milling process, but the grain should be rinsed again at home before using. It's important not to overcook quinoa because the moisture inside the tiny balls will cause them to explode. When this happens, the grain becomes an uninteresting, flat shell. Cook it similarly to rice, with a liquid to grain ratio of 2:1. Usually, depending on altitude, it cooks for 12 to 15 minutes.

Quail Salad with Damiana Vinaigrette

When my dad dined at The Fort, he always ordered this salad as a special request. He also reveled in telling our customers that Colorado's population had grown over the last 40 years due in large part to The Fort serving the Mexican herb, damiana, in our salad dressing. It is supposed to be a potent aphrodisiac!

SERVES 4

Ingredients

4 cups mixed salad greens

1 ripe avocado, peeled, pitted, and cut into narrow wedges

1 tablespoon small capers

1 tablespoon beni-shoga (kizami-shoga) (red pickled ginger)

¼ cup cubed jicama

1 12-ounce jar marinated artichoke hearts, cut into small pieces

1–1¼ cups Damiana Vinaigrette (page 100)

1 recipe William Bent's Teriyaki Quail (page 158)

GARNISH

1 medium tomato, cut into wedges

8 large radish crowns

½ cup toasted cashews

4 lemon wedges

Directions

Toss the greens, avocado, capers, beni-shoga, jicama, and artichoke hearts with the dressing. Place the salad on individual plates or one large platter and arrange the quail on top. Garnish with the tomato, radishes, toasted cashews, and lemon wedges.

HOW TO ROAST NUTS AND SEEDS

Very simply, I spread the nuts or seeds in a dry frying pan, turn on the flame to medium-low heat, and watch very carefully. I stir the nuts or seeds constantly with a wooden spoon and after 3 to 5 minutes, depending on the pan's contents, they are roasted—or toasted. Seeds cook a little faster and some may only need 30 to 40 seconds to darken slightly and turn fragrant.

I don't use oil; there is enough oil in the nut or seed, but if you're in a hurry, put about a teaspoon of oil in the pan or spray it with flavorless vegetable oil. Heat the oiled pan first and then add the nuts or seeds. As the toasting begins, you will smell a wonderful aroma and watch the nuts or seeds turn golden brown or a shade or two darker than they were. Remove the pan from the heat when their color is still light because they continue to toast a little in the hot pan, even off the heat. If desired, sprinkle fine salt over them. I prefer unsalted nuts; they are so good au naturel!

Smoked Duck Breast Salad

with Bayou Avocado Dressing

When we first served this lovely salad at The Fort, we made it with smoked pheasant. Now we use smoked duck, which is a little easier to come by—unless you know a good pheasant hunter with a smoker. The duck is especially succulent and works beautifully with the other ingredients. If jars of quail eggs are not available, substitute 4 hard-cooked hen's eggs, cut into quarters. Don't use canned quail eggs, because the quality is poor.

SERVES 4

Ingredients

2 cups chicken broth

2 (6-ounce) smoked duck breast fillets (recipe follows)

4 cups mixed greens

1 recipe Bayou Avocado Dressing (page 101)

2 cups sliced pickled beets

4 hard-cooked large hen's eggs

4 tablespoons lightly toasted pine nuts, for garnish

4 tablespoons currants, for garnish

8 fresh onion rings, for garnish (optional)

16 hard-cooked pickled quail eggs

12 radish crowns

Directions

1. In a wide skillet, bring the chicken broth to a simmer over medium heat. Add the duck breasts and cook gently for 5 to 10 minutes or until warmed through. Drain and slice the meat into ¼-inch-thick slices.

2. Toss the mixed greens thoroughly with the Bayou Avocado Dressing, then divide equally among four dinner plates. In the center, overlap 6 slices of pickled beets to make a ring and place a whole hen's egg in the middle. Arrange the slices of smoked duck breast on the beets, leaving visible the white top in the center of the hard-cooked egg.

3. Garnish the salad with toasted pine nuts and currants. A few rings of fresh onion are a nice addition, if desired. Arrange the quail eggs around the edge of the plate with the radishes.

Smoked Duck Breast

Ingredients

1 tablespoon brown sugar

1 tablespoon kosher salt

3 tablespoons hot water

2 (6-ounce) boneless duck breast fillets

1 applewood or hickory aluminum foil smoking bag (see "Where to Find It!")

Directions

1. Mix the brown sugar, salt, and hot water until the salt and sugar are dissolved to make a brine. Place the duck in a shallow pan and add the brine and enough cold water to cover the duck. Let the duck sit, covered, overnight in the refrigerator.

2. Preheat the oven to 250°F. Remove the fillets from the brine and place in the smoking bag. Fold the end of the bag to seal. Place the bag on the middle rack of the oven and smoke 35 minutes for rare, 40 minutes for medium, and 45 minutes for well done.

3. Let the duck rest in the bag for 5 to 10 minutes. Open the bag carefully to avoid being burned by the hot steam. Remove the skin from the fillets and discard. Slice the breasts and serve.

PICKLED DEVIL'S CLAWS

We used to eat these at home and at the restaurant, but, alas, our supplier, Dexter Hess, no longer can provide them. This story from my dad gives one insight into how much history and a sense of adventure inspired my family. Here's what Dad wrote: *In the summer of 1845, Lieutenant James Abert, a West Point grad, spent some time at Bent's Fort and kept a journal documenting the flora and fauna. Several entries concern a plant with large seedpods called Martynia proboscidea, or devil's claws. He wrote that when pickled, these pods resembled pickled okra and were good to eat.*

In the late 1980s, a retired botanist named Dexter Hess read these journals and went in search of devil's claws on the prairies south of La Junta, Colorado. Picking the seedpods at just the right time of year wasn't an easy task. Early August is a hot time in Colorado; the plant is not much more than two feet tall, and more than a few rattlesnakes inhabit the plains. But Dexter and his wife gathered enough for some experiments. Pickled, the little pods were delicious, and I commissioned him to pick and pickle devil's claws for The Fort.

They should be picked in late July or early August when the pods are young and before the antennae have formed and hardened. Using a long pin to probe the pods before picking is the best way to check for a tender tip. If hardened, the sharp hook (the devil's claw, no doubt) may cut your mouth. Still, it's a good idea to eat them carefully because it's nearly impossible to tell if the pods will be soft all the way through.

Pickled devil's claws have a slightly crunchy, sour pickle taste and the seedpod and antennae are tasty as well as fun to eat. I keep a secret store of them to feed adventurous eaters.

Fort Green Salad with Pickled Ginger, Jicama, and Pepitas

My dad loved all the flavors and textures found in this salad, as do I. We have made it for years and serve it with every meal at The Fort as part of the price of the entrée. It's never extra, although we keep adding "extras" to the mix to make this salad the best there is. The last flavor delight my dad added was in 1999 when he discovered peppadew peppers, introduced to him by our close foodie friend Suzanne Roser.

SERVES 4-6

Ingredients

2 cups cubed herb bread

2 tablespoons olive oil

⅓ cup grated Parmigiano-Reggiano cheese

1 tablespoon raw or roasted hulled pumpkin seeds (pepitas)

6 cups mixed fresh salad greens (mesclun)

1¼–1½ cups favorite Fort salad dressing

½ cup finely diced jicama

12 slices tomato or 24 cherry tomatoes, halved

3 teaspoons beni-shoga (kizami-shoga) (red pickled ginger)

12 pickled, hard-cooked quail eggs (see Note)

4–6 peppadew peppers, diced (see Note)

1 recipe Smoked Duck Breast (page 95) (optional)

Directions

1. Preheat the oven to 350°F. Toss the bread cubes with the olive oil. Arrange in a single layer in a baking dish. Bake for about 8 minutes, until golden but not dry, then toss with the cheese. Set aside.

2. If you use raw pepitas, roast them in a dry skillet over medium heat, shaking it periodically until they begin to pop.

3. To make the salad, toss the greens with the salad dressing and divide among chilled salad plates or shallow bowls. Add, in order, the jicama, pepitas, tomato, beni-shoga, quail eggs, and peppadew peppers. Sprinkle the croutons on the top. To make this an entrée salad, top with smoked duck breast sliced ¼ inch thick.

Note: Look for jarred quail eggs; the canned Asian variety are not very good. Peppadew peppers are the sweet/hot pickled red peppers sold at olive bars in grocery stores.

Heirloom Three Sacred Sisters Salad

The ancient Native Americans knew a thing or two about sustainable agriculture, as evidenced by how they cultivated three of their most important crops: corn, beans, and squash. They called these foods "the three sacred sisters" because the plants protected and nurtured one another as they grew. The corn was planted in a mound of earth and the beans were planted in a circular pattern around the cornstalks. Finally, the squash seeds circled the beans. As the plants grew, the beans climbed up the cornstalks and the squash leaves shaded the tender tendrils put out by the beans. Perfect symbiosis! With this colorful and delicious salad, we pay tribute to the sacred sisters. Be sure to say a blessing to them before eating it.

SERVES 4–6

Ingredients

2 tablespoons unsalted butter

1 chayote squash, diced

¼ cup white wine vinegar

Juice of ½ lemon

2 tablespoons sugar

1 tablespoon minced fresh tarragon or ½ teaspoon dried tarragon

3–5 tablespoons olive oil

Salt and freshly ground black pepper, to taste

1½ cups fresh or frozen corn kernels, blanched and drained

1½ cups cooked Anasazi beans, or pinto beans, rinsed

1 green bell pepper, seeded and diced

1 red bell pepper, seeded and diced

4–6 sprigs fresh cilantro, for garnish

⅓ cup hulled sunflower seeds, lightly toasted, for garnish

Directions

1. In a skillet over medium-high heat, melt the butter. Add the diced chayote and sauté for 2 to 3 minutes, until slightly softened and beginning to brown.

2. In a salad bowl, combine the vinegar, lemon juice, sugar, and tarragon. Gradually whisk in the olive oil. Taste and season with salt and pepper. Add the corn, beans, squash, and bell peppers. Toss the salad, then chill for 1 hour in the refrigerator. Serve garnished with fresh cilantro and toasted sunflower seeds.

VINAIGRETTES AND DRESSINGS

We assemble and dress our salads just before serving at The Fort, which is how they should be made at home, too. While you may opt to wash the greens and cut up many of the ingredients ahead of time, don't mix the salad until you are just about ready to carry it to the table. Drizzle it with the dressing and gently toss it. Hold the ingredients at room temperature before throwing them together; icy cold green salads are not very good. Don't saturate the greens with the salad dressing or you will be in for unappetizing, soggy leaves. Use a light hand but one that ensures all the ingredients are lightly coated and flavored.

We make several dressings and vinaigrettes at The Fort. While vinaigrettes can fall into the category of dressing, I separate them here based on their texture. In my book, dressings are a little creamier and denser than vinaigrettes, which are lighter mixtures primarily of oil and vinegar. We have served all these at various times during our history. For instance, the Bayou Avocado Dressing was on our original menu in the 1960s but is not now, although I think we will bring it back for our 60th anniversary celebration in a few years. My dad loved the Damiana Vinaigrette, made with an herb he found in Mexico and always claimed was an aphrodisiac. It takes some advance planning, but once you make it, you'll love it. Our blue cheese dressing, made with irresistibly sharp Maytag blue cheese, is addictive. Maytag is a domestic blue and well worth locating. And, yes, in case you were wondering, the same family that made the washing machine also figured out how to make sublime blue cheese.

Chipotle Honey Vinaigrette

Everyone loves this salad dressing, developed by our former executive chef Dave Woolley. Its happy notes of hot pepper and sweet honey mingle uproariously with fresh vegetables, and the mayonnaise smooths it out so that it's about as satisfying as any dressing can be.

MAKES ABOUT 1¼ CUPS

Ingredients

1 chipotle chile en adobo (canned)

1–2 tablespoons adobo sauce, to taste

¼ cup honey or agave nectar

1 cup mayonnaise

1–1½ tablespoons white distilled vinegar, to taste

Salt, to taste

Directions

In a food processor, purée the chipotle with the adobo sauce. With the machine still running, slowly add the honey. Stop the machine and add the mayonnaise and vinegar. Pulse on and off until the dressing is smooth. Add salt to taste.

Damiana Vinaigrette

The Fort's most popular vinaigrette dressing. Damiana is an herb from Mexico and is a reported aphrodisiac! My dad claimed that the population of Colorado grew by the thousands, due to so many guests enjoying a Fort salad dressed with Damiana herb vinaigrette.

MAKES ABOUT 2 CUPS

Ingredients

½ cup red wine vinegar

1 tablespoon water

¾ teaspoon dried damiana (see "Where to Find It!")

1½ cups salad oil

1 tablespoon sugar

Salt and freshly ground white pepper, to taste

Directions

1. Heat the vinegar and water in a nonreactive saucepan to almost boiling, about 190°F. Add the damiana and mix well. Place the vinegar mixture in a sealed glass container and set aside at room temperature for 2 weeks.

2. Pour the mixture through a strainer to remove the leaf. Whisk in the oil, sugar, and salt and white pepper. Taste and adjust the seasonings.

Bayou Avocado Dressing

My mother Bay developed this dressing recipe for The Fort in the 1960s. It was served in the early years at The Fort as a delicious dressing for chicken or shrimp salad.

MAKES ABOUT 1¼ CUPS

Ingredients

¾ cup mayonnaise

½ cup buttermilk

2 tablespoons tarragon vinegar

1 tablespoon snipped fresh chives or minced green onions

1 tablespoon minced Italian parsley

1 tablespoon minced fresh tarragon leaves or ¼ teaspoon dried

1 small clove garlic, minced

3–5 canned flat anchovy fillets, rinsed and chopped

Salt and freshly ground black pepper, to taste

Directions

In a small mixing bowl, whisk together the mayonnaise, buttermilk, vinegar, chives, parsley, tarragon, garlic, and anchovy fillets. This dressing should be just thick enough to cling to the lettuce, but not heavy. Taste and add a little more vinegar and buttermilk, if needed. Season to taste with salt and pepper.

Chunky Maytag Blue Dressing

The Fort is known for serving the BEST blue cheese. In the 1960s, we discovered the American blue cheese company, Maytag, which has produced a wonderful blue cheese on the Maytag Dairy Farms, outside of Newton, Iowa, the former home of the Maytag Corporation, since 1941. You may have had a Maytag washing machine years ago. This is the same family that produces Maytag blue cheese today!

MAKES ABOUT 1¾ CUPS

Ingredients

1 cup mayonnaise

½ cup full-fat sour cream

¼ cup milk

½ teaspoon Worcestershire sauce

½ teaspoon freshly ground white pepper

1 clove garlic, crushed

¼ teaspoon salt

1½ teaspoons chopped fresh thyme

⅓ cup crumbled Maytag blue cheese, with some larger pieces

Directions

Place all the ingredients except the blue cheese in a blender or food processor and pulse on and off until smooth. Stir in the blue cheese by hand. Cover the dressing and refrigerate overnight to allow the flavors to blend. The dressing may be stored for up to 2 weeks in the refrigerator.

Jalapeño Buttermilk Ranch Dressing

A creamy buttermilk dressing with a kick! My mother Bay developed this recipe in the 1960s. It has been a favorite on our menu for over 50 years!

MAKES ABOUT 1½ CUPS

Ingredients

1 fresh jalapeño chile

¾ cup mayonnaise

½ cup sour cream

¼ cup buttermilk

¼ cup diced red bell pepper

2 tablespoons chopped green onion

2 tablespoons chopped Italian parsley

1 tablespoon chopped fresh basil

1 tablespoon chopped fresh cilantro

1½ teaspoons chopped fresh thyme

1 large clove garlic, peeled and minced

⅛ teaspoon dried dill seed (optional)

3–6 drops hot sauce, to taste (optional)

3–6 drops Worcestershire sauce, to taste

Salt and freshly ground black pepper, to taste

1 tablespoon fresh lime juice

Directions

Seed and dice the jalapeño. In a blender or food processor, combine the diced jalapeño, mayonnaise, sour cream, buttermilk, bell pepper, green onion, parsley, basil, cilantro, thyme, garlic, and dill seed, if using. Pulse on and off until the dressing is well blended and almost smooth. Taste and season with the hot sauce (if using), Worcestershire, salt and pepper, and lime juice.

Vegetable Side Dishes

The Fort's Famous Black Beans

When we opened in the early 1960s, there were very few dishes on the menu that included legumes such as black beans. At the time, most Americans may have been somewhat familiar with pinto or kidney beans but knew very little about any others. In those early days, Luis Bonachea was our manager and, being from Cuba, he insisted that black beans, cooked in the Cuban style, were the Rolls Royce of all beans. Our customers agreed with him and since then we have served these black beans, made from a recipe Luis shared with us from his homeland. They are never off the menu; our loyal followers would be decidedly unhappy if we decided to omit them!

SERVES 8

Ingredients

4 cups black beans (sometimes called turtle beans)

6 quarts water

2 yellow onions, finely chopped

4 cloves garlic, crushed

3 ham hocks

4 green bell peppers, seeded and chopped

4 bay leaves

½ teaspoon powdered cloves

½ teaspoon whole black peppercorns

1 cup olive or salad oil

1 cup white vinegar

Salt, to taste

Directions

1. Rinse the beans thoroughly, checking for rocks or gravel. Soak them overnight in enough water to cover them by 4 inches. The next day, drain and rinse the beans; place them in a stockpot and add 6 quarts of water. (Using fresh water helps the beans not be as musical—flatulence producing—as they might be.)

2. Add the onions, garlic, ham hocks, bell peppers, bay leaves, cloves, and peppercorns. Cover, bring to a boil, and then simmer for 3 to 5 hours, until tender. Check on the beans frequently, and if the liquid level has dropped so as to threaten to expose the beans, add more hot water. (Always add hot water, never cold, to beans during cooking; cold water makes them tough.) Keep the heat low and stir occasionally to prevent burning.

3. When the beans soften, remove the ham hocks and separate the meat from the bone. Chop the meat into bite-size pieces and add to the beans. In the last hour of cooking, add the oil and vinegar. Season to taste with salt just before serving.

Heirloom BBQ Beans

Dave Woolley, our former executive chef, came up with this recipe for barbecued beans. Dave and my dad shared a love of beans, and this dish, using heirloom beans, quickly became a great favorite of Dad's.

SERVES 8

Ingredients

16 ounces dried heirloom beans (Anasazi, Zuni Gold, Colorado River, or Scarlett Runner beans or a combination of varieties)

1 (19-ounce) bottle Jack Daniel's Original BBQ Sauce

1 (18-ounce) bottle Kraft Spicy Honey BBQ Sauce

½ cup Mae Ploy sweet chili sauce

¼ cup brown sugar1 large clove garlic, minced

1½ teaspoons ground cumin

1½ teaspoons dried Mexican oregano

1½ teaspoons ground paprika

1½ teaspoons mild to medium ground New Mexican red chile

1½ teaspoons kosher salt

1 teaspoon chile caribe (crushed red chiles)

½ teaspoon freshly ground black pepper

3 slices applewood smoked bacon, diced

1 cup chopped yellow onion

½ pound roasted, diced buffalo or beef

Directions

1. Pick over and rinse the beans. Soak them overnight in enough water to cover by 4 inches. If using more than one variety, soak the beans in separate containers.

2. Drain and rinse the beans and place them in a heavy-bottomed pot with enough water to cover by 4 inches. If using more than one variety, cook the beans separately (different beans have different cooking times). Bring the water to a boil over high heat. Cover and reduce the heat to low. Simmer the beans for 2 to 4 hours, stirring occasionally, until tender. If necessary, add additional hot water so that the beans remain covered.

3. Meanwhile, in a mixing bowl, combine the barbecue sauces, chili sauce, and brown sugar. Stir in the garlic, cumin, oregano, paprika, ground chile, salt, chile caribe, and black pepper. Set aside.

4. In a large skillet, over medium-low heat, cook bacon until crisp. Add the onion and cook until slightly caramelized. Set aside.

5. Drain the cooked beans, reserving the cooking liquid. Place the beans in a large heavy-bottomed pot. Add the sauce mixture, sautéed bacon and onion, and the buffalo or beef roast. Mix together gently. Reheat the barbecued beans over medium to low heat, adding 2 to 6 cups of the reserved hot bean broth if the mixture seems to be getting dry. Serve hot.

Bay's Georgia Green Chile Grits

My mother, Bay, was a born-and-bred southerner who developed a great love of the West. She moved back to Georgia after she and my father divorced but always kept a foot in both places. When I visited her once in 2003, she was working as a historian-interpreter at a living-history farm in Tifton, Georgia, called Agrirama. At the farm, they ground local corn and grits between huge millstones from the 1880s. I asked if they could supply The Fort with the grits, and to this day we are fortunate enough to get stone-ground grits from Georgia, the best you'll ever taste! My mom prided herself on her dishes made with grits and this is a standout. Mom's ashes are now buried next to the big red rock outside The Fort, but she lives always through her famous grits. We give them a western twist with the addition of Monterey Jack, Colby, and asadero cheese.

SERVES 4–6

Ingredients

3 slices applewood smoked bacon, diced

½ cup finely chopped yellow onion

2 poblano chiles, roasted, peeled, seeded, and diced

1 clove garlic, minced

1 cup heavy whipping cream

3 cups chicken broth

1 cup old-fashioned, long-cooking stone-ground hominy grits (see Note)

¾ cup grated mixed cheeses, such as Monterey Jack, Colby, and asadero

Salt and freshly ground black pepper, to taste

Directions

1. In a large, deep sauté pan, over medium-low heat, cook the bacon until crisp, 2 to 3 minutes. Add the onion and sauté until translucent, 2 to 3 minutes. Add the chiles and garlic and cook for 1 minute.

2. Stir in the cream, broth, and grits. Bring to a simmer over medium heat, stirring frequently. Reduce the heat to low and cook, stirring frequently, 20 to 30 minutes, until the liquid is absorbed and the grits are thick and creamy. Remove the grits from the heat and stir in the cheeses. Season to taste with salt and pepper. Serve immediately.

Note: If old-fashioned, long-cooking grits are not available in your area, use quick-cooking grits—not instant grits. Allow the broth and cream to simmer for 10 minutes before adding the grits. Cook the grits for about 5 minutes, until thickened and creamy, and then stir in the cheeses. The texture will not be the same as with long-cooking grits, but it will be acceptable in a pinch.

Chayote Squash

This ancient squash was first cultivated in Mexico, where it was a great favorite of the Aztecs and Mayans, but now is grown in most warm regions stretching across our hemisphere. It's even found its way to Europe, where it rates as an exotic vegetable. The French and French Caribbeans called it christophene. Some people call it a vegetable pear because of its size and shape. When chayote is cooked correctly, it has an appealing texture—like water chestnuts—and deep, starchy flavor. We cook it simply, and it's one of our most popular vegetable dishes. When you buy chayote, refrigerate it and cook it soon after purchase. It's not quite as sturdy as some other squash.

SERVES 4-6

Ingredients

2 chayote squash

3 tablespoons unsalted butter

⅔ cup thinly sliced scallions

2 roasted red bell peppers, cut into small dice

2 tablespoons minced fresh cilantro

Salt and freshly ground pepper, to taste

Directions

1. Cut the chayote in half lengthwise. Slice the halves lengthwise into ¼-inch-thick slices. Cut the slices lengthwise into thin strips.

2. Place a large skillet or sauté pan over medium-high heat and add the butter. When the butter melts and the foam begins to subside, add the scallions, roasted peppers, chayote, and cilantro. Sauté about 2 minutes, until the squash is tender-crisp. Season with salt and pepper and serve.

Carrots or Beets with Red Chile Honey Glaze

When fall comes to the Rocky Mountains and the aspens shimmer gold in the crisp air, we turn to harvest vegetables for inspiration. Few dishes are better than this, made with the season's best freshly dug carrots or beets. Both turn wonderfully sweet when roasted, and when helped along with red chile honey, they are gloriously sweet, hot, and sour with undertones of fruit. Everyone loves these, from our most discriminating guests to the kids who walk through our doors.

Red chile honey is sold in some supermarkets, but you can easily make it yourself by stirring some pure New Mexico chile powder into mild honey. The chile powder has a lovely sweet-and-hot quality without being overpowering. As an aside, chile honey is an ancient remedy for mouth pain. It doesn't cure a sore but relieves the pain.

This is an easy dish to make because the vegetables can be roasted ahead of time and then cooked for a few minutes to glaze and reheat.

SERVES 4–6

Ingredients

2 to 3 cups raw carrot slices, cut diagonally ¼ inch thick, or 4–6 medium-size fresh beets

1 recipe Red Chile Honey Glaze (page 62)

Salt and freshly ground black pepper, to taste

Red chile honey (page 62), to taste

Directions

1. If you are using carrots, boil them in water until barely tender, about 5 minutes. If you are using beets, cut the stems to 1 inch and leave the root ends intact (this helps keep them from bleeding). Boil them, covered, for 30 to 40 minutes or until tender.

2. When the carrots are done, toss them in the glaze to coat thoroughly, reheating if necessary. For beets, run them under cold water, remove the root and stem ends, and pull off the skins. Drain well. Slice, dice, or cut the beets into julienne strips and toss them in the glaze to coat thoroughly, reheating if necessary.

3. Adjust the seasoning, adding salt and pepper and red chile honey to taste.

Zuni Succotash with Toasted Sunflower Seed Hearts

Succotash is truly a Native American dish, always made with beans and corn. No one in Europe had heard of it, nor had they heard of the ingredients common in succotash, until Christopher Columbus dropped anchor in the Caribbean in the 15th century. Most culinary historians trace the dish's roots to the Narragansett tribe, who lived in the Northeast, where it was a simple dish of corn, lima beans, and fish. Further inland, Native Americans made similar dishes with beans, corn, and bear fat. At The Fort, we substitute Anasazi beans for the more familiar lima beans and add sunflower seeds, too. This is to honor the Zunis, whose reservation in northern Arizona is surrounded by the far larger Navajo res.

SERVES 4–6

Ingredients

½ cup raw or roasted sunflower seed hearts (hulled sunflower seeds)

2 cups frozen lima beans or 1 cup dried Anasazi beans

2 strips bacon

2 cups fresh sweet corn, cut from the cob (about 3 ears), or frozen or canned whole kernel corn

1 medium yellow onion, finely chopped

1 cup canned, chopped mild green chile

1 small red bell pepper, seeded and finely diced

1 small green bell pepper, seeded and finely diced

Directions

1. If using raw sunflower seed hearts, toast them in a small dry skillet over medium-low heat, stirring until lightly browned, about 5 minutes. If using frozen lima beans, set them aside to thaw. If using Anasazi beans, soak them overnight in cold water, then drain, rinse, and boil in fresh water for 2 to 3 hours, until soft and mealy.

2. In a large skillet, cook the bacon over medium-low heat until crisp. Remove and drain on paper towels. Sauté the corn and onion in the bacon drippings for about 3 minutes. If you prefer, use vegetable oil instead of the bacon fat. Add the beans, green chile, red and green bell peppers, and sunflower seeds and sauté, over medium heat, until the bell peppers are slightly softened and the onion is translucent. Sprinkle crisp bacon over the hot succotash and serve.

Spaghetti Squash with Garden Mint

When the mint is fresh in the markets or growing rampant in your backyard, make this amazing side dish. It's one of my favorites, and I particularly like it with Herbed Lamb Chops (page 179) or Tarragon Gazpacho (page 85).

SERVES 4–6

Ingredients

1 small spaghetti squash (about 4 pounds)

4 tablespoons unsalted butter, softened

⅓ cup fresh mint leaves, finely chopped, or 2–3 teaspoons dried mint

Salt and freshly ground black pepper, to taste

½ cup grated Parmigiano-Reggiano cheese (optional)

Directions

1. With a large, heavy chef's knife, cut the squash in half lengthwise. Scrape out the seeds and strings.

2. To cook in the oven: Preheat the oven to 375°F. Place the squash halves cut side down in a shallow roasting pan. Add enough water to the pan to come up 1 inch from the sides. Cover the pan tightly with aluminum foil. Bake for 40 to 50 minutes, until the squash is tender when pierced with a knife. Set aside for 15 minutes to cool.

3. To cook in the microwave: Place the squash halves cut side down in a microwavable glass dish large enough to accommodate both halves. Add 1 cup of water; cover with microwavable plastic wrap and place in the microwave. Cook on high for 7 minutes. Check to see if the squash flesh is tender. If the flesh is still hard, microwave a few minutes more. Carefully remove the dish from the microwave and let the squash rest for 15 minutes to cool and continue steaming.

4. With a fork, scrape the strands of squash into a large pasta bowl or colorful serving dish. Add the butter and chopped mint. Season generously with salt and pepper. Add the grated cheese, if using. Toss gently. If the squash has cooled, pop it in the microwave for 2 to 4 minutes before serving.

Zucchini and Yellow-Neck Squash with Heirloom Tomatoes

This is the perfect late-summer side dish to serve alongside grilled meat or chicken. Zucchini is sometimes called green summer squash, and yellow-neck squash is nothing more exotic than yellow summer squash. What you call them depends on where you live. Heirloom tomatoes are sold at many farmers' markets and you may even grow them in your backyard garden, as I do. If you can't find them, never mind. Use any fresh, vine-ripened tomatoes.

SERVES 4-6

Ingredients

4 tablespoons unsalted butter

2 tablespoons olive oil

1 white or red onion, peeled and chopped

1 clove garlic, peeled and minced

1 zucchini squash, washed and sliced into ¼-inch-thick rounds

1 yellow-neck squash, washed and sliced into ¼-inch-thick rounds

¼ cup dry vermouth

2-3 large heirloom tomatoes, blanched, peeled, seeded, and chopped

¼ cup finely chopped fresh herbs (parsley, thyme, and basil) or 2 teaspoons dried herbes de Provence

Salt and freshly ground black pepper, to taste

Directions

1. Heat the butter and olive oil in a sauté pan or large skillet. Add the onion, garlic, and squashes and sauté over medium-high heat, allowing them to caramelize, for 6 to 8 minutes.

2. Add the dry vermouth to deglaze the pan. Add the chopped heirloom tomatoes, herbs, and salt and pepper. Cover with a lid and cook for 2 minutes more. Remove from the heat and serve.

Shoepeg Corn with Sweet Peppers

Shoepeg corn is nearly always sold in cans or frozen these days. Evidently it was quite popular in the South before the Civil War, but after that cultivation dropped off and it is now hard to find—except in cans or frozen in butter. My dad loved it because it reminded him of growing up in Pennsylvania (which is hardly the Deep South, but evidently his mother bought it regularly and cooked with it). I "cheat" a little with this recipe and use fresh corn cut from the cobs, but if you prefer to use the real thing, buy canned or frozen shoepeg. To most closely approximate shoepeg corn kernels, look for ears of sweet, white corn with small kernels. The corn got its name because the little kernels resemble the tops of wooden pegs that cobblers used to attach soles to the upper parts of shoes long ago. At The Fort we add chopped serrano chiles to the recipe to "give it authority!" This is a quick and easy recipe that can be completed in 25 minutes.

SERVES 4–6

Ingredients

4 cups corn kernels (approximately 6 ears; see Note)

1 cup diced red bell pepper

1–2 serrano chiles, diced (see Note)

3 tablespoons unsalted butter

Salt and ground white pepper, to taste

Directions

Heat the corn in a large saucepan over medium heat, with the bell peppers, chiles, and butter until the peppers have softened just a bit and the corn is heated through. Approximately 10-15 minutes. Season to taste with salt and pepper.

Note: Fresh corn is best, of course. To remove it from the cob, use either a very sharp knife or a special tool made for removing it. This tool, which has a sharp metal ring with handles like ears on either side, runs down the cob neatly and quickly. Shoepeg corn is commonly available frozen in butter sauce; if you use this, you need not add extra butter. If you use canned corn, drain it first. For a milder dish, remove the ribs and seeds of the serrano chiles before dicing.

Cha Cha Murphys

It's not surprising that potatoes were dubbed "Murphys" in the 19th century, as a nod to the large numbers of Irish immigrants who moved West. They often stayed west of the Mississippi after serving in the army or ended up in Colorado or a neighboring state in search of work. Given that the region was also heavily influenced by Mexican cooking, hot salsa cruda was often mixed into potatoes to jazz them up a little. At The Fort, we make a twice-baked potato with salsa. It's been on the menu for years and judging by how much our customers like it, it won't be removed anytime soon.

SERVES 6

Ingredients

4 (8-ounce) russet potatoes

½–¾ cup light cream

½ cup salsa cruda

1½ cups grated cheddar cheese

½ cup grated Parmigiano-Reggiano cheese

Directions

1. Peel and quarter the potatoes. Cover them with cold water in a large pot, bring to a simmer, and cook 20 to 30 minutes, until a knife can easily be inserted. When the potatoes are done, drain the water and return the potatoes to the pan, placing it over very low heat to evaporate the last of the water. This takes just a minute or two and gives you fluffier potatoes.

2. Preheat the oven to 350°F.

3. If you really want to build your arm strength, mash the potatoes with an old-fashioned masher and a colander. I prefer to use a potato ricer, which squeezes the potato through small holes.

4. In a small saucepan, bring the cream just to a simmer over medium heat (don't boil it). Add the cream, salsa cruda, and cheddar cheese to the mashed potatoes and stir well.

5. Pipe or spoon the potatoes into individual ramekins or a 9-inch square casserole. You can use the back of a spoon to raise the potatoes up into small peaks that will brown nicely. Sprinkle with the grated Parmigiano-Reggiano cheese and bake for 20 minutes. Serve immediately.

San Luis Fingerling Potatoes

If you aren't familiar with fingerling potatoes, here is a good way to try them. They are small, knobby potatoes that tend to be long and narrow, hence the name, with a lovely sweetness. While fingerlings are usually white potatoes, they also can be blue. They are small and thin-skinned but are not new (immature) potatoes and so have a more complex flavor. Fingerlings are grown in Colorado's San Luis Valley, which is also known for its quinoa and blue Peruvian potatoes. It's no surprise these crops do well here; we share the same high altitude as Peru.

SERVES 4–6

Ingredients

1 pound fingerling potatoes, washed but not peeled

4 cups chicken broth or water

1 tablespoon olive oil

1 small white or red onion, chopped

Salt and freshly ground pepper, to taste

¼ cup whipped butter, softened

¼ cup sour cream

1 teaspoon dried dill weed

Directions

1. Boil the fingerlings in chicken broth or water in a medium sized saucepan for 20 minutes or until tender when speared with a fork.

2. While the potatoes are cooking, prepare the onions. In a skillet, heat olive oil; add onions and sauté over medium heat until lightly browned and caramelized, 2 to 3 minutes. Sprinkle the onions with salt and pepper and set aside. When the fingerlings are cooked, drain them well.

3. In a small mixing bowl, whisk together the whipped butter, sour cream, and dill. If the mixture remains lumpy, microwave for 10 seconds, then whisk until smooth and fluffy. Gently fold in the onions. If necessary, warm the potatoes over low to moderate heat on the stove. Serve topped with the whipped butter/sour cream sauce.

Fort-Style Red Potatoes with Corn and Anasazi Beans

Looking for something to serve with a big, juicy, charred buffalo steak? At The Fort we serve all our steaks with this glorious potato-and-corn dish. We get our potatoes from Colorado's fertile San Luis Valley, although I suggest you use the freshest, most locally grown red potatoes you can find.

SERVES 6-8

Ingredients

1 cup dried Anasazi beans, soaked for at least 2 hours

1½ pounds small red potatoes, quartered

4 tablespoons unsalted butter

¼ cup canola oil

½ cup finely chopped yellow onion

1 teaspoon seasoned salt

½ cup white shoepeg corn (fresh, frozen, or canned)

1 fresh green chile, diced (Anaheim preferred)

½ cup diced red bell pepper

¼ cup chopped Italian parsley

½ teaspoon toasted canola seeds (optional)

Directions

1. Drain the beans and place in a saucepan. Cover with fresh water and bring to a boil, and then lower the heat to a brisk simmer until the beans are soft, about 2 hours. Drain and set aside.

2. Preheat the oven to 400°F.

3. Boil the potato quarters in salted water for 20 to 30 minutes or until easily pierced with a knife, then drain well and bake on an ungreased baking sheet for 15 minutes; the bottoms will brown a bit.

4. In a large sauté pan, melt butter with the oil over medium-high heat. When quite hot, add the onion and sauté for about 4 minutes, until lightly browned. Add the seasoned salt, corn, green chile, and red bell pepper. Cook for 2 minutes, then add the potatoes, beans, and parsley. Stir gently until well combined and heated through. Serve with a sprinkle of the canola seeds.

Irish Trappers Champ

During the last few years of his life, Dad insisted we add this dish to the menu. And so we did, much to the delight of our guests. Dad had researched a potato dish called champ that was introduced to the American West in the 19th century by Irish immigrants. At The Fort, we serve it as a side dish, although it used to be a main dish, too. It's simple mashed potatoes enriched with lots of butter, cream, and green onions (also known as scallions). In some recipes, each forkful of potato is dipped in melted butter. Talk about rich! Colcannon is a related potato dish made with shredded, cooked cabbage stirred into the potatoes.

SERVES 4–6

Note: You can also use 1½ cups of chopped kale or spinach in place of the scallions. Delicious!

Ingredients

2–2½ pounds red potatoes

½–¾ cup half-and-half or light cream

6 tablespoons unsalted butter, divided

1⅓ cups chopped scallions (1 large bunch)

Salt and freshly ground pepper, to taste

Directions

1. Peel the potatoes and cut into 2-inch pieces. Cook potatoes in boiling salted water until tender, 12 to 15 minutes. Drain. Meanwhile, in a large, deep skillet or sauté pan, combine the half-and-half and 4 tablespoons of butter. Add the scallions and bring to a simmer over medium heat. Reduce the heat to low and cook gently for 2 to 4 minutes.

2. Add the potatoes to the cream sauce, and season generously with salt and pepper. Stir until the potatoes are heated through and well coated. Spoon the potatoes into a serving bowl, and top with the remaining butter. Serve at once.

THE HISTORY OF RICE IN THE SOUTHWEST

When most people think of western cooking, they don't think of rice. They may conjure up meals heavy with potatoes, biscuits, and corn, but rice is not something that immediately springs to mind. Of course, when you think of Mexican food, rice is front and center, and so it stands to reason it would be a familiar ingredient in the food of the Southwest.

The Spanish brought rice to the New World in the 1500s and watched the crop flourish. The conquistadores, who spent much time in Mexico, thought of New Mexico and Colorado as the northern frontier. When they ventured north, they packed rice in their saddlebags because it was easy to carry, easy to cook, and always filling. By the 1800s, rice was common in the West. It was served at Bent's Fort, and many a beaver trapper cooked it over a campfire deep in the Rocky Mountain woodlands.

Arroz con Huevos Duros

When she was a 19-year-old bride in 1846, Susan Shelby Magoffin and her husband, Samuel Magoffin, set off down the Santa Fe Trail, which, unlike the Oregon and California Trails, was strictly a trade route. Although the couple had honeymooned for six months in Philadelphia and New York, the trip west particularly excited Susan. Her trader husband, who was 27 years her senior, made sure the journey was as luxurious and comfortable as possible for his new wife—for instance, every night a group of workers pitched a special tent and set up an actual bed with a mattress, sheets, blankets, and pillows. Susan, who was born in Kentucky to a wealthy family, was eager to keep a journal of her travels, a diary that was first published in 1926 by Yale University and called *Down the Santa Fe Trail and into Mexico*. In the journal, Susan speaks of stopping at Bent's Fort, where the party waited for American soldiers to ensure their safe passage to Santa Fe. Susan was charmed by the Mexicans she met along the way and tried to learn to speak Spanish. She was especially impressed with the food and in the journal describes a large bowl of rice with hard-cooked eggs. My father researched this dish, among others, and found it was sometimes called *sopa seca*, or dry soup. In this recipe the rice is very moist, almost like a risotto, and could be served as a meatless main course or a side dish.

When I reviewed the original journal at the Beinecke Library at Yale, I was thrilled to discover more than 50 pages of poetry. The Tesoro Cultural Center will publish the poetry of Susan Shelby Magoffin in the very near future.

SERVES 4-6

Ingredients

2 tablespoons olive or canola oil

1 ripe tomato, finely diced

1½ cups finely diced yellow onion (1 medium)

½ teaspoon dried Mexican leaf oregano

½ teaspoon salt

½ cup chopped green chiles (canned work well)

1 cup long-grain rice

2 cups low-sodium chicken broth

3-4 hard-cooked large eggs

Sprinkling of New Mexican ground red chile, for garnish (optional)

Fresh cilantro or Italian parsley sprigs, for garnish (optional)

Directions

1. Place oil in a large, deep skillet or sauté pan over medium-high heat. When the oil begins to smoke, add the tomato, onion, oregano, salt, and chiles. Stir quickly until the onions are translucent and the tomatoes have browned a little. Add the rice and chicken broth. Bring it to a boil, stirring.

2. Reduce the heat to low, cover, and don't peek for 25 minutes.

3. Spoon the rice onto a serving platter and garnish with the eggs, cut in half lengthwise and placed yolk side up. A dash of red chile dusted across the top makes for a wonderful presentation, with little sprigs of parsley or cilantro growing from the dish.

Rice Pilaf

At The Fort, we make rice pilaf with basmati rice from Pakistan, although American-grown basmati is also very good. We make the pilaf with a mixture of rice and quinoa, with the latter providing nuttiness and chewy texture. We also stir in dried barberries, currents, or cranberries. This lightly flavored pilaf is one of the best.

SERVES 6-8

Ingredients

1 cup basmati rice, well washed 6 times

8 strands saffron

½ cup dried currants

2 tablespoons barberries (see Note)

1 cup quinoa

½ cup pine nuts, lightly toasted

¼ cup finely diced red bell pepper

¼ cup finely diced green bell pepper

½ cup flavorful olive oil

Salt and white pepper, to taste

Note: Barberries, which are dried, may be found in Middle Eastern groceries. Dried cranberries or dried sour cherries make interesting and flavorful substitutes and may be easier to find. At The Fort we use one-third cooked quinoa to two-thirds rice. You may want to experiment to see how you like to balance the flavors. Mushrooms or mushroom stems are an excellent addition. Sauté them and add them along with the peppers.

Directions

1. Rinse the rice in 6 changes of cold water. Simply place the rice in the rice cooker with 2 cups water, saffron, currants, and barberries. If you don't have a rice cooker, place the same ingredients in a wide 3-quart (or more) cooking pot with a lid. Bring to a boil, uncovered, and then turn the heat to low and simmer, covered, for about 20 minutes. Keeping the lid on, turn off the heat and let the rice steam for another 10 minutes, then open and fluff with a fork.

2. While the rice is cooking, prepare the quinoa. Properly cooked quinoa has a wonderful texture, almost like caviar but without the fish taste. It has a slightly bitter taste, but the commercial milling process usually eliminates most of it. Rinse the grain with cold water in a chinois (conical sieve), pushing your hand back and forth in it as the water pours through. Any remaining soapy dust will wash away, and your quinoa will taste its best.

3. Cook the rinsed quinoa in two parts water to one part grain. It will take about 12 to 15 minutes, depending on your altitude (far less time than the rice), so begin making it after the rice starts cooking. Don't cook the quinoa longer than it takes to soften and swell into ball-shaped grains. Cooks who leave quinoa unattended will find that the grains have gotten too hot and have popped and become flat, not nearly as good to eat.

4. Empty both the rice and the quinoa into a large bowl. Using two forks, gently fold in the pine nuts, peppers, and olive oil. Because the peppers are finely diced, the heat of the rice will slightly soften them. Add salt and pepper to taste.

Wild Mushroom Risotto

Risotto is an irresistibly creamy rice dish that really shines when cooked with care at home. It demands time spent standing over the hot stove and stirring, but is well worth it. This one is filled with "wild" mushrooms, which are not really wild but cultivated forest mushrooms with deep, earthy flavors. Try to use Italian arborio, carnaroli, or vialone nano rice if possible. These medium-grain imported rice varieties have high starch contents, and the starch dissolves as the rice cooks to help form the creamy sauce.

SERVES 4-6

Ingredients

3 tablespoons unsalted butter

1½ cups chopped yellow onion (1 medium)

2 cups sliced wild mushrooms (cremini, oyster, shitake, and porcini)

2 cups white arborio rice

8 cups low-sodium chicken broth

½ cup dry white wine

1½ teaspoons concentrated mushroom bullion base (optional)

1 cup grated Parmigiano-Reggiano cheese

Salt and freshly ground pepper, to taste

Directions

1. Place the butter in a large, deep sauté pan over medium heat. When the butter melts and turns clear, add onion and mushrooms. Cook, stirring for about 2 minutes, until the onion turns translucent and the mushrooms are lightly browned. Add rice and sauté for 2 minutes, until coated with butter.

2. Meanwhile, in a large saucepan, bring the chicken broth to a simmer. Set aside.

3. Add the wine to the rice mixture and stir until the rice absorbs it. Stir mushroom base, if using, into the broth. Slowly, in 1 cup increments, add hot broth to the rice, stirring over medium-low to low heat, until the rice absorbs the liquid. This should take about 20 minutes.

4. When all of the broth has been absorbed and the rice is creamy and tender, but still slightly firm, stir in the grated cheese. Season with salt and pepper and serve immediately. Risotto may be served as a main course or as a side dish.

Breads from the Oven

Indian Horno Bread

We developed this bread to resemble bread baked in a horno oven. It's not the same, of course, but will give you an idea of how amazing that bread, cooked at a relatively high temperature, tastes.

MAKES 2 LOAVES

Ingredients

1 tablespoon (1¼-ounce package) active dry yeast

¼ cup lukewarm water

4½ tablespoons melted lard or shortening, divided

4½ cups sifted all-purpose flour

1 teaspoon salt

1 cup water

Directions

1. In the bowl of a stand mixer with a dough hook attachment, dissolve the yeast in the ¼ cup of lukewarm water. Let stand until the yeast foams, about 5 minutes. Mix in 2 tablespoons of the melted lard or shortening, blending thoroughly. Sift together the flour and salt, then add the flour mixture and 1 cup of room temperature water alternately, mixing until a smooth dough forms.

2. Place the dough in an oiled bowl, turning once so that the top is oiled. Cover with a damp cloth and let rise until double in size, about 1 hour. Two fingers stuck into the dough will leave impressions.

3. Preheat the oven to 400°F. When the dough has doubled, punch it down and knead it vigorously on a lightly floured board for at least 5 minutes. Shape into two balls and place on a greased baking sheet. Brush the loaves with remaining melted lard or shortening and let them rise in a warm place for 15 minutes. Bake for 50 minutes or until the loaves are lightly browned.

Herb Bread

A bread seasoned with no fewer than five different herbs and garlic is sure to get your senses going. We served this at The Fort throughout the 1990s with soups and salads, and it still finds its way onto our menu from time to time.

MAKES 2 LOAVES

Ingredients

1 tablespoon (1 ¼-ounce package) active dry yeast

1 tablespoon sugar

1 cup lukewarm water

2 tablespoons vegetable oil

3–3½ cups all-purpose flour

1 teaspoon salt

1 teaspoon garlic powder

1 teaspoon ground oregano

1 teaspoon dried leaf oregano

1 teaspoon dried thyme

1 teaspoon dried rosemary

1 tablespoon dried dill weed

2 tablespoons dried parsley

Sprinkling of cornmeal

Directions

1. In a large mixing bowl, dissolve the yeast and sugar in the lukewarm water. Add the oil. In a separate bowl, stir together the flour, salt, and herbs. Add to the yeast mixture and mix thoroughly to form a soft dough.

2. Place the dough in an oiled bowl, turning once so that the top is oiled. Cover with a wet cloth and let rise in a warm place until double in size, about 1 hour.

3. Punch the dough down and let it rise again, for about an hour. This helps develop the flavor of the yeast. Turn out onto a floured board. Shape into two 12-inch French loaves and place them on a greased cookie sheet that has been sprinkled with cornmeal. Slash the tops diagonally. Cover and let rise again for another hour, or until double.

4. Heat oven to 350 degrees. Bake for 25 to 30 minutes, until golden.

Ranch-Style Pan Bread

This quick bread is easy to make and has a light, cakey texture. When folks traveled west on wagon trains, they did not have ovens to bake bread and so devised ways to make bread in deep pots and skillets. Germans, many of whom were from Pennsylvania and called Pennsylvania Dutch, are responsible for the term "Dutch oven" as a pot for baking.

SERVES 4-6

Ingredients

2 cups sifted all-purpose flour

3 teaspoons baking powder

1 teaspoon salt

6 tablespoons vegetable shortening

1¼ cups milk

Directions

1. Preheat the oven to 450°F.

2. Combine flour, baking powder, salt, and shortening in a food processor, and pulse on and off until the mixture has the texture of coarse meal. Add milk and pulse on and off until dough comes together, being careful not to overmix. The dough will be quite sticky.

3. Spread the dough into a 9-inch greased, heavy iron skillet and bake for 25 to 30 minutes or until deep golden brown. Trust your eyes, not the clock, to tell you when this bread is done. For crustier bread, spread the dough more thinly in a 10-inch greased iron skillet and bake until deep golden brown.

Jalapeño Cornbread

This bread is one of the most-requested dishes at The Fort, and for good reason. We spike it with jalapeños and enrich it with coconut milk, admittedly not a common ingredient in the Old West! Indigenous people across the continent introduced settlers from Europe to corn and all its uses, and so today, cornbread is as commonplace in New England as in New Mexico. I love this bread with a hearty soup or stew.

SERVES 6

Ingredients

1 tablespoon plus 1½ teaspoons vegetable oil, divided

1 cup yellow or white cornmeal

1 cup all-purpose flour

¼ cup sugar

2½ teaspoons baking powder (reduce to 1½ teaspoons at high altitudes)

1 teaspoon salt

2 large eggs

2 cups coconut milk

⅓ cup minced fresh jalapeños, seeds and ribs removed

½ cup well-drained golden corn kernels (canned)

Directions

1. Preheat the oven to 350°F. Grease a 9-inch heavy cast-iron skillet or square baking pan with 1½ teaspoons vegetable oil.

2. In a large mixing bowl, stir together cornmeal, flour, sugar, baking powder, and salt. In a separate bowl whisk together eggs, coconut milk, jalapeños, corn, and remaining tablespoon of oil. With a wooden spatula, mix wet ingredients into the dry ingredients until just combined.

3. Pour batter into the prepared skillet and place on middle rack of the oven. Bake for about 45 minutes, until bread is a pale golden brown. Do not overbake. Serve cornbread warm, with sweet butter.

Bannock Bread with Dried Western Fruits

Bannock bread is another easy quick bread developed to be cooked in whatever pan was handy and often on top of the stove or over a campfire, although in this recipe, it's baked in the oven. It's thought of as a western bread since the pioneers made it on the trail and once they homesteaded; thus it's also called bush bread or trail bread. Bannock was one of the first homemade breads we served at The Fort in 1963 when we opened, and although I was a child, I have fond memories of waiting for it to be pulled, piping hot, from the oven. I loved to break a piece off the loaf and smell the aroma of warm dried fruits and yummy bread.

SERVES 6

Ingredients

5⅓ tablespoons unsalted butter, melted

2 cups all-purpose flour

2 teaspoons baking powder (reduce to 1½ or 1 teaspoon at high altitudes)

½ teaspoon salt

2½ teaspoons sugar

⅓ cup sweetened dried cranberries

⅓ cup dried blueberries or currants

¾ cup milk

Directions

1. Preheat the oven to 350°F. Brush the bottom and sides of a 9-inch heavy iron skillet or 8- to 9-inch shallow baking pan with butter. Reserve remaining butter.

2. Sift flour, baking powder, and salt into a medium mixing bowl. Stir in sugar and dried fruit. Add milk and remaining butter and stir with a wooden spatula to form a moist, but not sticky, dough.

3. Gently press the dough into the buttered skillet. Bake on the middle rack of the oven for about 30 minutes, until loaf is golden brown. Serve bannock warm, with sweet butter.

Note: For the bread to show a deep, golden brown top, brush 2 tablespoons of melted butter or egg whites on top of the bread loaf just before baking.

Lakota Indian Fry Bread

We serve Indian fry bread at the Tesoro Cultural Center's annual Indian Market held in early June, following a recipe very similar to this one. It's for basic bread dough leavened with baking powder. The dough is formed into flat rectangles or disks and cooked in hot lard. The process is quick and uncomplicated, and the crispy, light bread makes a marvelous treat.

SERVES 4-6

INDIAN FRY BREAD, IN SAM ARNOLD'S WORDS

It's not known exactly when or how fry bread came to the Plains Indians. It was certainly not until they had metal kettles for frying and that was after trade began with whites. There is no indication that frying in pottery or on a hot rock was part of the pre-Columbian culture, and so it stands to reason that the cooking method was probably introduced to the Indians in the form of German or Dutch settlers' doughnuts, called "oily cakes."

This recipe was first prepared for me in 1969 by a woman from the Brule tribe, a branch of Sioux Indians in South Dakota. I was visiting the Rosebud Sioux Indian Reservation to film traditional American Indian dishes for my PBS series Frying Pans West.

The woman prepared the dough by hand, mixing dry ingredients in a bowl and then beating in small amounts of water with a long wooden spoon until a moist but firm dough had formed. After kneading it well, she rolled out a grapefruit-size ball of dough with a piece of broom handle to about half an inch thick and cut it into pieces measuring about four-by-five inches. Pueblo Indians, on the other hand, traditionally make disks with three-quarter-inch holes punched through in their centers. The hole serves two purposes: It allows the hot fat to flow through and cook the top surface of the bread; it allows for easy removal when the bread is done.

In South Dakota, the baker dropped the dough pieces into an iron kettle filled with very hot, nearly smoking melted pork lard and immediately began spooning hot fat over the dough. The resulting steam inside the dough caused it to puff it up beautifully. We ate the fry bread with honey or sprinkled with cinnamon sugar, both traditional toppings.

Ingredients

1 quart tallow, lard, or canola oil for deep-frying

1¾ cups all-purpose flour

1½ teaspoons baking powder

¾ teaspoon salt

Honey or cinnamon sugar, for serving

Directions

1. Heat the oil in a deep pot to 380°F. The best flavor comes from either beef tallow (rendered beef fat) or lard, but with today's food fashion, health-conscious people use canola oil.

2. The easiest way to make fry bread is with a dough hook attachment on an electric mixer. In the mixer bowl, thoroughly combine flour, baking powder, and salt. Add ¾ cup water, and mix until a supple, uniform dough forms. Add more water if needed to achieve a dough that is not too sticky but not too dry.

3. Divide dough into 4 to 6 equal portions, and form into rounds. Roll out the rounds on a floured surface to a thickness of between ½ and ¼ inch. If you'd like to try Pueblo-style fry bread, use your finger to make a ¾-inch hole in the center of each piece of dough.

4. If you don't have a thermometer to check the heat of your oil, carefully lower a small piece of dough into the hot oil. It should blister and puff up instantly. Fry two to three pieces per batch. In the first few seconds of frying, use a spoon to pour fat over the bread to make sure all surfaces fry immediately. Remove and drain on a paper towel. Allow a full minute between batches to bring the oil back up to temperature.

5. Many people dip fry bread in honey or bite a hole in the side and squeeze honey into the center. Others sprinkle cinnamon sugar on it. Whatever your pleasure, the most important thing about fry bread is that it must be eaten hot, immediately after it's cooked.

Pumpkin-Walnut Muffins

A 1975 Fort menu reads: "The pumpkin-nut muffins are a closely guarded secret; the recipe is asked for nightly but never revealed." Finally, the secret is out! Turns out, it's all about the pumpkin. These muffins contain nearly twice as much as other recipes. Because of this, they're cooked for a relatively long time at an unusually low temperature and turn out especially dense, moist, and flavorful.

MAKES ABOUT 2 DOZEN MUFFINS

Ingredients

2½ cups all-purpose flour

½ cup sugar

1¼ cups powdered milk

2 tablespoons ground cinnamon

1½ teaspoons salt

¾ cup brown sugar

¾ cup chopped walnuts

2 large eggs (size does make a difference)

¾ cup vegetable oil

⅔ cup water

1 (29-ounce) can pumpkin (not pie filling)

Directions

1. Preheat the oven to 325°F. Grease 3-inch muffin tins or line with paper baking cups.

2. In a large mixing bowl, combine flour, sugar, powdered milk, cinnamon, salt, sugar, and walnuts. In a separate bowl, whisk together eggs, vegetable oil, water, and pumpkin. Mix the dry and wet ingredients together until just combined. The batter should be easy to scoop. If it is too thick, add a little more water.

3. Fill the muffin cups three-quarters full and bake for 40 to 45 minutes. Let the muffins cool before removing them from the pan. Because they are so moist, these reheat beautifully.

PUMPKINS IN THE WEST, IN SAM ARNOLD'S WORDS

The bright orange pumpkins dotting the fields throughout Colorado played a great role in the state's history. The first domesticated pumpkin was grown in 7000 BC in Mexico's northeastern Tamaulipas region. Seeds were traded to other tribes, and by 3000 BC, pumpkins had traveled to Puebla, Mexico. Within another 500 years, pumpkins had journeyed as far as Peru.

Pumpkins traveled north, too. The basket makers in Colorado's Durango and Mesa Verde areas grew them before AD 400. The Indian diet consisted of corn, beans, and various squashes, including our common pumpkin. When the fur trappers arrived in the region in the early 1800s, pumpkin became a major part of their diet. Mountain men such as Kit Carson, Uncle Dick Wootton, and others who frequented the original Bent's Fort were familiar with pumpkin.

On an 1842 visit to Colorado's Fort Lancaster (later Fort Lupton), Rufus Sage [told] of a trading party of Mexicans from Taos who brought with them pack horses and mules laden with corn, bread, beans, onions, and dried pumpkin to barter for the buffalo robes, furs, guns, and tobacco sold at The Fort. Today thousands of pumpkins are grown near Fort Lupton.

Quinoa Muffins

Quinoa contains more usable protein than any other grain, and it is said that a man can easily work a 12-hour day on one cup of it. So far, this claim has gone unproven at The Fort; with so much great food around, who can stop after a single cup of quinoa? We have an accommodating and faithful staff, but none of them has volunteered to test it. Regardless, these healthful muffins with undertones of orange are divine: nutty, a little crunchy, and just a tiny bit sweet.

MAKES 1 DOZEN MUFFINS

Ingredients

2 large eggs

½ cup canola oil

½ cup brown sugar

⅓ cup honey

1 teaspoon baking soda

½ teaspoon orange oil or 1½ teaspoons finely grated orange peel

¾ cup quinoa flour

½ cup all-purpose flour

¼ cup wheat germ

2 tablespoons yellow cornmeal

¾ teaspoon baking powder

½ teaspoon salt

¼ cup canola seeds (poppy seeds may be substituted)

½ cup coarsely chopped walnuts, toasted

¼–½ cup milk

Directions

1. Preheat the oven to 375°F. Grease a 3-inch muffin pan or fill it with paper liners.

2. In a mixing bowl, combine the eggs, oil, sugar, honey, baking soda, and orange oil, blending thoroughly. Add both flours and the wheat germ, cornmeal, baking powder, salt, canola seeds, and walnuts. Mix well and add ¼ cup milk. If the batter seems too dry, add an additional ¼ cup milk. The batter should be thick but pourable.

3. Fill muffin cups three-quarters full and bake for about 20 minutes, until golden brown.

Bay's Southern Spoon Bread

My mother, Bay, may have adopted Colorado as her home for many years, but she was a southerner, born and bred in Georgia and part of a family with roots dating back to the early 18th century. This recipe was first written down in the 1700s and passed down through the generations until it landed in my mother's childhood kitchen. In a lovely ostrich leather–bound notebook, Mom wrote down this and many other recipes in her clear, beautiful handwriting. Most were accompanied with a few lines of family history; for example, this bread is meant to be served on Sunday evening "with a silver spoon, of course." It goes without saying that I treasure this small book. I adore the spoon bread's pure cornmeal flavor and custard-like texture. My husband prefers it flavored with cheese or spices; I like it best with cane syrup, molasses, or raw honey.

SERVES 4–6

Ingredients

1½ tablespoons unsalted butter, divided

2 cups half-and-half or whole milk

1 cup white or yellow cornmeal (preferably stone ground)

3 large eggs, separated

1 teaspoon baking powder

1 teaspoon salt

Cane syrup, molasses, or honey, for serving

Directions

1. Preheat the oven to 350°F. Generously butter an 8-inch shallow baking dish that can be brought to the table. Reserve the remaining 1 tablespoon butter.

2. In a large saucepan, over medium heat, bring the half-and-half almost to a simmer. Gradually stir in cornmeal, whisking constantly until the mixture begins to thicken, 2 to 3 minutes. Off the heat, whisk in the egg yolks, one at a time, and then the baking powder, salt, and remaining butter.

3. In the clean bowl of an electric mixer, beat the egg whites until they stand in stiff peaks. Fold the beaten whites into the cornmeal mixture.

4. Pour batter into the prepared baking dish. Bake 35 to 45 minutes, until the spoon bread has risen and is beginning to turn golden. Serve as soon as possible, with a silver spoon, of course! Drizzle with cane syrup, molasses, or honey.

Variation: Cheddar and Ham Spoon Bread. To the recipe above, add ¼ teaspoon freshly ground pepper, ¼ teaspoon freshly grated nutmeg, ⅛ teaspoon cayenne pepper, 1 cup shredded sharp cheddar cheese, and ¾ cup chopped ham. Prepare the cornmeal batter as described in the master recipe, adding pepper, nutmeg, and cayenne with the salt. Fold cheese and ham into the warm cornmeal mixture. Fold in the stiffly beaten egg whites and bake as described above. Serve this savory spoon bread as a light main course, accompanied by a green salad.

Meats of the Great Plains

World's Best Beef or Buffalo Prime Rib Roast

We've been serving juicy buffalo prime rib since the 1960s and our customers have always loved it. We roast it surrounded by the skins and outer layers of multiple onions, which impart amazing flavor to the meat as they smoke and char in the oven. When I was a little girl, the aroma of roasting buffalo and caramelizing onion literally made my mouth water. When the roast comes to the table, you might be tempted to shout "Hip, hip, huzzah!"—and for good reason!

SERVES 8–10

Ingredients

1 (5- to 6-pound) beef or buffalo standing prime rib roast or 1 (4- to 5-pound) boneless prime rib roast

½ cup beef base concentrate (available at meat markets and specialty stores)

¼ cup freshly puréed garlic (about 2 heads)

½ cup dried rosemary

Coarsely ground black pepper

¼ cup vegetable oil

Outer peels of 4 large onions

Directions

1. Rub the roast with the beef base concentrate and then the garlic. Sprinkle the rosemary and pepper over all, letting it stick to the beef base. Wipe the oil on your hands and gently rub the seasonings into the roast. Let stand for 1 hour at room temperature.

2. Preheat the oven to 500°F. Place the roast on a foil-covered roasting pan. Arrange the onion peels around the base of the roast and place the pan in the oven. Roast for 8 minutes, so that the onion peels burn and the smoke lightly penetrates the meat.

3. Lower the heat to 250°F. Roast for 18 minutes per pound or until a meat thermometer reads 125°F for rare or 138°F for medium-rare. The low temperature will keep the roast tender. Don't cook buffalo any longer; because of its leanness, it will be tough if cooked more than medium-rare.

4. Remove the roast from the oven and allow it to rest for 15 to 20 minutes before carving. The temperature will rise about 10 degrees, bringing the meat to the correct serving temperature.

Buffalo Nutrition Information

(mg/100 grams)	Protein	Fat	Calories	Cholesterol
Buffalo ribeye	22.2	2.2	148	61
Beef choice ribeye	22.0	6.5	180	72
Skinless chicken breast	23.6	0.7	167	62
Pork ribeye	22.3	4.9	165	71

William Bent's Herb Butter Buffalo Tenderloin Filet Mignon

In my opinion, this is the best meat in the house. Clearly a lot of others feel the same way, as we sell more than 70,000 buffalo entrées every year, and 70 percent of those are tenderloin. Recently, a guest approached me and announced that he was from Paris, France. "All my life I have thought that Chateaubriand was the ne plus ultra of cuts," he said, "but now I must return to France and tell my friends that Chateaubriand is garbage. The best meat in the world is buffalo tenderloin." Need I say more?

In 2019 our chef, Mike Winkler, created a sizzling buffalo tenderloin in herb butter seared and served on a cast-iron platter . It was such a hit that this preparation is now the most popular tenderloin steak at The Fort. Everything is better with butter!

Make sure your butcher cuts away the tough, sinewy strap running along the tenderloin. This makes the cut look almost square. It should be about 1 to 1½ inches thick. You don't need more than 8 ounces, unless you are very hungry!

SERVES 1

Ingredients

TENDERLOIN

1 tablespoon olive oil

4 tablespoons unsalted butter

¼ teaspoon fresh thyme

½ tablespoon minced garlic

Salt and pepper, to taste

Buffalo filet mignon (your choice of size)

1 garlic clove, smashed

1 sprig rosemary

ACCOMPANIMENT

4 tablespoons unsalted butter

1 red onion, julienned

1 cup of shitake mushrooms

2 tablespoons brown sugar

Salt and pepper, to taste

1. Heat a cast-iron skillet or cast iron 9" pan on high. Add olive oil, unsalted butter, fresh thyme, minced garlic, and salt and pepper to the skillet. Place the steak, garlic clove, and rosemary in the skillet and cook the meat to your desired doneness, about 3 minutes per side for rare and 4 minutes per side for medium-rare. Be careful not to overcook, as the skillet will continue to cook the steak off the heat.

2. As the steak is cooking, heat a sauté pan over medium heat, melt butter and add onions, mushrooms, brown sugar, and salt and pepper.

3. Cook over medium heat until the mushrooms and onions have reduced and caramelized, approximately 5-10 minutes. Serve with the steak on the cast iron skillet. If you don't have a skillet, you can prepare in a cast iron pan, and serve on a heated dinner plate with the onions and mushrooms.

Herb Butter

This delicious herb butter compound has multi-uses at The Fort. It's great on steaks, dinner rolls, or even scrambled or fried eggs!

MAKES 1 POUND

Ingredients

2 tablespoons chopped shallot (1 medium)

2 tablespoons chopped Italian parsley

2 tablespoons chopped fresh basil leaves

1 tablespoon snipped fresh chives

1 tablespoon chopped fresh cilantro leaves

1½ teaspoons minced garlic (1 clove)

1½ teaspoons fresh thyme or ¼ teaspoon dried leaf thyme

1½ teaspoons fresh rosemary leaves

1½ teaspoons fresh lemon juice

1 teaspoon kosher salt

1 pound (4 sticks) unsalted butter, at room temperature

1-2 tablespoons dry white wine

1 teaspoon Worcestershire sauce

Directions

1. Place shallot, parsley, basil, chives, cilantro, garlic, thyme, and rosemary in a food processor. Pulse on and off until puréed. Add the lemon juice and salt.

2. Put the butter and herb purée in an electric mixer bowl and beat with the paddle attachment. Add wine and Worcestershire sauce and beat until all ingredients are fully incorporated.

3. Wrap the butter in plastic wrap, forming it into two logs, each about 2 inches in diameter. Store in refrigerator or freezer until firm. With a sharp knife dipped in cold water, cut off a ½-inch-thick

slice of herb butter to top a sizzling hot steak, warm piece of baked bread, or try it in scrambled eggs! Herb butter may be stored in the refrigerator for several days and in the freezer for up to 2 months.

Traditional Fort Preparation

If you want The Fort's traditional recipe for cooking buffalo tenderloin, here is Sam Arnold's version.

SERVES 1

Ingredients

½ teaspoon fine sea salt

⅛ teaspoon lemon crystals (citric acid or sour salt)

¾ teaspoon freshly ground black pepper

1 (8-ounce) buffalo or beef tenderloin steak (see Note)

1 tablespoon Canola oil

1 teaspoon minced Italian parsley (optional)

2 teaspoons Herb Butter (page 140) or plain unsalted butter

Directions

1. Preheat the broiler or heat a grill to medium high. Combine the sea salt, lemon crystals, and pepper. Dust the steak with this mixture, coating it liberally on both sides, and then brush lightly with oil. (The order is important here—no oiling before seasoning.)

2. Place the steaks about 6 inches from a medium-high fire. Cook for 11 to 18 minutes (depending on thickness) or until the meat is medium-rare. Turn every 4 minutes. Because buffalo is so lean, it tends to be tough when cooked more than medium-rare, so it's important not to overcook.

3. Sprinkle with the parsley, if using. A disk of herb butter gives this steak even greater magnificence. This is not precisely what the doctor ordered, but if your weight and cholesterol are fine, go for it every blue moon. It's worth a lot of penance. The smell of the butter melting on a hot steak is intoxicating.

Note: This recipe works beautifully with beef T-bone steaks, too. Splurge and buy the best beef you can, which means USDA prime meat, or a high grade of USDA choice, such as Angus. A thick T-bone—1 to 1½ inches—will probably result in leftovers, but since the meat makes great sandwiches, this is rarely a problem. If you cook thinner steaks, watch them very carefully so that they don't overcook. Porterhouse steak, which is similar to a T-bone, just with a bigger eye or tenderloin, works well for two servings. Cut the meat away from the bone before serving so that you can divide the tenderloin into two portions. Slice the strip side crosswise into an even number of pieces.

A SHORT HISTORY OF A BIG ANIMAL, IN SAM ARNOLD'S WORDS

Early writers tell us that Boston's crooked streets leading down to the Charles River originally were buffalo trails. The last bison east of the Appalachians was killed in about 1830, although by that time the great herds of the plains had hardly been touched by the relatively few Native Americans living there. Colorado, for example, was believed to be home to fewer than 8,000 Indians, and these were small bands of Cheyenne, Sioux, Arapahoe, Lakota, and Ute; just a few people in a territory the size of New Zealand and far fewer than go to a shopping mall on Saturday afternoon. The bison were far from endangered, and the Native Americans took only what they needed.

The Indian used every part of the carcass. Tongues, hearts, livers, kidneys, and testicles were removed for choice eating and the rest of the meat was sliced along the grain into thin sheets for drying to make jerky. Drying racks in Indian camps were always filled with meat, so necessary for winter stews made with dried squashes, cattails, prairie potatoes, wild onions, and garlic and dried maize. This stew was called washtunkala by the Sioux and is still eaten today. It's pretty good!

When the "white eyes," as the Indians called the white mountain men, went west, they learned Indian ways of cooking. Pieces of buffalo meat skewered on wood sticks were called buffalo en appolas and were broiled over open fires. Jerked buffalo meat was commonplace, too. Pounded with chokecherries and mixed with melted kidney fat, it formed a pasty mixture called pemmican and was the sustainable ration of both Native Americans and mountain men.

The ultimate delicacy was the buffalo tongue, which has a fine, smooth grain and delicate flavor. It was served by the train-car full at the finest restaurants in the nation. I've looked high and low for a 19th-century cookbook with recipes for buffalo or bison but can find none, although many letters and journals make references to eating it.

As trains crisscrossed the nation, train companies ran advertisements promising to "clean and dress the buffalo" if one of their passengers "bagged one." The train engineer would drive the locomotives into the middle of buffalo herds crossing the tracks and passengers could shoot them from the train windows. Not quite the same sport as riding bareback into the center of a herd with bow and arrow, pumping hunting arrows into fat young cows surrounded by mean old bulls! Low-paid buffalo skinners dressed the kills on the spot, salting the hides to preserve them until the mighty train hunter returned to St. Louis, where it was transformed into a buffalo robe for winter sleigh-riding comfort.

It is little wonder that by 1910 reports indicated that only 254 buffalo existed worldwide—and this count included a bison in a zoo in Calcutta, India. By the time James Fraser designed the Indian Head/Buffalo nickel, minted from 1913 until 1938, the white men had effectively wiped out the animals. In so doing, they stripped Native Americans of food, clothing, and shelter, efficiently destroying their way of life and forcing them to join the white man's world.

By the first half of the 20th century, bison became largely mythical creatures not only of the American West but of the past. Small herds were seen by lucky travelers to national parks such as Yellowstone in Wyoming.

I knew little about these animals in 1963 when I opened The Fort, but when I set out to learn all I could about the original Bent's Fort, I found that Kit Carson had had a contract with Bent, St. Vrain and Company to bring in 1,000 pounds of meat a day, and most of it was buffalo. I investigated serving buffalo and found several ranches in the western states. Instead of being extinct, I discovered that the herds were steadily increasing.

When we began offering buffalo, we had a hard time getting people to try it. "I'm not a tourist, I'm from around here and I've tasted buffalo," they'd say. "I'll stick to beef!" The attitude was understandable because quality was spotty and sometimes just plain bad.

Occasionally we'd get meat so tough it had to have come from an old cow. I quickly got to know my purveyors and since then we at The Fort have been insistent on getting nothing but the best meat from young bulls that are between 18 and 26 months old.

Today we serve buffalo tenderloin steaks, New York–style strip steaks, sirloin on a skewer, and roast prime rib. Appetizer plates include broiled split buffalo marrow bones, tongue, homemade sausage called "boudies," and testicles, also known as Rocky Mountain oysters.

By the dawn of the 21st century, buffalo numbered well over 350,000 in this country and herds are increasing quickly in size and number. Buffalo ranches exist in all 50 states, including Rhode Island. Countries such as Germany and Switzerland boast a few herds, too. The renaissance of the American bison is an important trend in food history. It's an essential part of our New World American heritage, truly a food of the Old West.

Gonzales Steak

Our customers love this steak, which has been on the menu since 1964—although its presence
was made possible only after a good-natured squabble between my dad and Elidio Gonzales, the
renowned wood carver from Taos, New Mexico, who was so important to The Fort in its early days (see
page 59). Here is how my father described the sequence of events that led to the creation of this
full-flavored steak dish.

*On April 1, 1964, Elidio Gonzales, the gifted Taos Madero (woodcraftsman) came to Denver to give wood
carving demonstrations at The Fort. When he called me from town for help, hopelessly lost among Denver's
one-way streets, I was tempted to repeat to him what he'd told me in late October after a heavy snowfall. At
that time, I had harangued him for being three months late finishing The Fort's doors. "People in Hell always
want ice water!" Elidio had said.*

*The adage about wanting what you couldn't have had taken the wind out of my sails and I had waited
patiently for another month before the doors arrived. Elidio now needed my help. As I drove to town and led
him back to The Fort, I pondered how I could teach him an April Fool's Day lesson. The solution came to me
when he asked for a steak with chiles.*

"This is no Mexican restaurant!" I thundered. "We don't have any chile here," I fibbed.

"Oh, you damned gringos, you don't know what's good," he replied. "All you eat is meat and potatoes!"

*I then went back to the kitchen, cut a pocket into a thick sirloin, stuffed it with chopped green chiles, and
grilled the steak. I placed it in front of a grumbling Elidio and watched him take a bite. "April Fool, Elidio!" I
shouted.*

*"April Fool to you, too!" he replied without missing a beat. "You're the bigger fool for not having this on
your menu!"*

*He was right, of course. The Gonzales Steak has happily and proudly been on the menu since. Elidio
passed away years ago, but his furniture and his steak live on.*

SERVES 1

Ingredients

3 green Anaheim chiles, roasted and peeled (canned will do, but fresh are best)

4 tsp salt, divided

1 clove garlic, chopped

Pinch of dried Mexican oregano

1 (10- to 12-ounce) thick-cut buffalo or beef steak (New York strip, top sirloin, or tenderloin)

1–2 teaspoons canola oil

1 tbs freshly ground black pepper

1 teaspoon unsalted butter (optional)

Directions

1. Slit the chiles to remove the seeds and chop 2 chiles into a fine dice. Mix with 2 tsp salt, garlic, and oregano. (New Mexicans traditionally like to leave a few of the seeds in the dish. "The seeds give it life," they say.) Reserve the remaining whole chile.

2. With a very sharp knife, cut a horizontal pocket into the steak. Stuff the chopped chiles into the pocket. Brush the meat and the remaining chile with oil. Grill the steak on both sides on a charcoal or gas grill at medium high heat, to the desired doneness. If using buffalo, cook 3 minutes per side for rare to medium rare. For beef, cook 5 minutes per side for rare to medium rare. Buffalo contains less fat, so buffalo cooks much faster than beef and is best medium-rare.

3. Use the remaining 2 tsp salt and 1 tbs of pepper, sprinkle on the meat. Grill the remaining whole-roasted chile to get a nice patterning of grid burn on it. Lay it across the steak as a garnish. A teaspoon of brown butter drizzled over the steak as a special treat is heaven. To make brown butter, simply place the butter in a sauté pan over medium-high heat and allow it to melt and turn golden brown.

GRADING BEEF

The USDA grades the beef everyone buys. To qualify as prime beef, the meat must have a significantly high ratio of fat to meat—the result of feedlot fattening. Less than 2 percent of the beef sold in the United States is prime, which makes it hard to find. Below prime is choice, which is also very good beef, although the top levels of choice beef are better than the lower ones. Most shoppers end up with choice beef, which is never a bad thing. Below choice is select, and below that are industrial cuts rarely, if ever, seen by consumers.

Angus is a top-grade choice, as are some others. The best bet when buying meat is to find a butcher you can trust and stick with him or her. You may not have a butcher shop in your city or town, but talk to the guys behind the meat counter at the local supermarket. They usually are only too glad to help you choose the best meat for your needs.

Uncle Dick's "Incorrect" Buffalo or Beef Steak

My dad named this steak, first focusing on the "incorrect" part, because while he deemed this meal as glorious as a first kiss, it includes egg and cheese, two foodstuffs that should not be eaten with beef if you care about your cholesterol or your diet in general. But where's the fun in that? Every now and again, nothing is better! We like to honor historic figures at The Fort who we imagine would like our food. We named this for Richens "Uncle Dick" Wootton, a mountain man of yore who is perhaps best known for establishing the first toll road in Colorado along the Santa Fe Trail. When you travel south today on I-25, near Raton you still cross over Wootton's Pass (today it is called Raton Pass), but the toll is gone. A steak as decadent as this one perhaps needs a toll! Serve this with a side of Fort-Style Red Potatoes with Corn and Anasazi Beans (page 117).

SERVES 1

1 (8- to 12-ounce) buffalo or beef sirloin steak, cut 2 inches thick

2 tbs canola oil

Char Crust dry-rub seasoning (see "Where to Find It!") or salt and freshly ground black pepper

1 large egg

¼ cup shredded sharp white cheddar cheese

¼ cup Red Chile Sauce (page 60)

1. Lightly coat the steak with canola oil and generously season it with Char Crust or salt and pepper.

2. Cook the steak over high heat on a charcoal grill (with mesquite) or a gas grill for 6 to 8 minutes per side for medium-rare.

3. While the steak is grilling, cook the egg sunny-side up on a griddle or in an egg pan. When the steak is ready, top it with cheese, Red Chili Sauce, and the egg.

HOW TO COOK A BUFFALO

Hardly any other cut of meat compares to a good "buff tender," which is what we call tenderloins. The texture of buffalo is similar to beef except that it is less fatty. Its taste is slightly sweeter than beef and has been likened to beef injected with extra beef flavoring.

Since the best meat comes from young bulls between 18 and 26 months old, the body weight of a dressed carcass runs between 550 and 650 pounds, most of it bone and lesser cuts. This is easy to understand if you picture the buffalo on the Indian Head/Buffalo nickel. The head and shoulders are large, but the hind end is small and scrawny. Since the steaks come from the small end, this translates to about 11 to 12 pounds of tenderloin from a single 550-pound carcass. This explains why it is costly to produce.

Cooking buffalo is much like cooking beef, except that since it is extremely low in fat, when it's grilled it should be kept rare or medium-rare to avoid toughening. Slow oven roasting is best for prime ribs because the low temperatures will not drive off all juices and fat. If you marinate or braise the meat, use acidic liquid such as wine, beer, vinegar, yogurt, or citrus juices, which tenderize the meat by softening the collagen in the cells.

Smokehouse Buffalo BBQ Ribs

When Bobby Flay visited The Fort to film his television show, we featured these ribs, which Chef Flay declared were the best he had eaten all year! High praise indeed, but no surprise, as they are great favorites with us, too. Our very creative chef Dave Woolley came up with the recipe, which relies on a lip-smacking barbecue sauce made with Jack Daniel's whiskey. Buffalo ribs are larger than beef ribs and harder to find. Don't forgo this recipe because you can't find buffalo ribs; substitute beef or baby back pork ribs instead.

SERVES 4–6

Ingredients

1 cup Jack Daniel's or bourbon

1 cup molasses

½ cup orange juice concentrate

¼ cup whole garlic cloves, peeled and crushed with flat side of chef's knife

¼ cup fresh thyme sprigs or 1 teaspoon dried leaf thyme

2 bay leaves

1½ teaspoons salt

3 cups water

5 pounds buffalo (or beef or pork) back ribs

Hickory wood smoking chips or 2–3 hickory aluminum foil smoker bags

Directions

1. In a large nonreactive saucepan, combine Jack Daniel's, molasses, orange juice concentrate, garlic, thyme, bay leaves, salt, and water. Bring to a boil over medium-high heat, stirring often. Reduce heat to low and simmer gently, stirring occasionally, for 20 minutes. Meanwhile, preheat the oven to 200°F.

2. Place the ribs in a large shallow braising pan and pour the braising liquid over them. Cover the pan tightly with aluminum foil. Braise in the oven for 6 to 8 hours, until very tender.

3. Remove ribs from the liquid and allow to cool. Pour the liquid through a strainer into a saucepan. Cook over medium-low heat, stirring often, for 8 to 10 minutes or until the liquid is reduced to about 1 cup. Reserve this liquid to add to the barbecue sauce. Increase the oven temperature to 450°F.

4. Smoke the ribs over hickory chips on a grill, or in hickory aluminum foil smoker bags on the bottom rack of the oven, for 1 hour. On the grill, baste with Jack Daniel's BBQ sauce (page 53) during the last 15 to 20 minutes. If using smoker bags, baste with the sauce after smoking is complete.

Elk Chops St. Vrain

Our famous Game Plate, a very popular dish at The Fort, includes these chops. It also boasts William Bent's Buffalo Tenderloin (page 139) and Teriyaki Quail (page 158). Ceran St. Vrain, a French nobleman, founded the trading business Bent, St. Vrain and Company in the 1830s, and his family were original settlers in St. Louis.

SERVES 4

Ingredients

1 (2- to 3-pound) Cervena (elk) rack cut into 8 bone-in chops

¼ cup canola oil

4 tablespoons Char Crust dry-rub seasoning (see "Where to Find It!") (optional)

Salt and freshly ground pepper, to taste

1 cup huckleberry preserves

Directions

1. Lightly coat the chops with canola oil and season both sides with 1 tbs Char Crust (if using) per chop (or 1 tsp salt and 1 tsp pepper per chop in place of Char Crust).

2. Grill over high heat, 3 to 5 minutes per side for medium-rare.

3. Serve 2 chops per person with 2 to 3 tablespoons of warm huckleberry preserves.

Buffalo Blue Corn Tamale Pie

Chances are you are familiar with blue corn chips and blue corn tortillas, but if you haven't tried blue cornmeal in a tamale pie such as this one, you don't know what you are missing. Many Indians and other southwesterners still use the meal ground from dark-colored corn into cornmeal called *maiz azul*.

SERVES 6

Ingredients

1–2 tablespoons olive or canola oil

1 pound coarsely ground beef or buffalo chuck

1½ cups chopped yellow onion (1 large)

2 cloves garlic, peeled and minced

1½ teaspoons dried Mexican oregano

½ teaspoon fennel seed, crushed

1 teaspoon salt, divided

2 cups pine nuts or coarsely chopped walnuts

⅓ cup Red Chile Purée (page 59)

2 quarts chicken broth

2 cups blue cornmeal

½ cup cold water

1 cup medium whole pitted ripe black olives, divided

2 cups grated sharp cheddar cheese, divided

Garnish

½ cup each red and green bell pepper strips, cut attractively (optional)

1 avocado, sliced (optional)

¼ cup toasted pine nuts or whole walnut halves (optional)

4 tbs chopped parsley or cilantro

GREEN RIVER KNIVES

Green River skinning knives make great steak knives, which is why we sell them at The Fort in the Trade Lodge. The knives have been made by the Russell Harrington Cutlery Company in Massachusetts since 1834, when they were mostly used by trappers and hunters. Kit Carson carried a Green River knife—and that's a good enough recommendation for us. When we first opened, customers bought a steak knife, which we kept for them until they returned and needed to use it. Today, our guests can purchase the knives and take them home.

Directions

1. Wipe a large skillet with oil and brown the meat in small batches over high heat, removing to a bowl as each batch is cooked. Cooking too much meat at once will steam it rather than brown it.

2. In the same pan, over medium heat, cook the onion, garlic, oregano, fennel, ¼ teaspoon salt, and nuts for 3 to 5 minutes, stirring often, until onion is softened and lightly browned. Add this mixture to the meat and stir in the Red Chile Purée (page 59).

3. Bring the chicken broth to a boil in a large stockpot. (The cornmeal will bubble and splash if the pot isn't deep enough.) While the broth is heating, combine the blue cornmeal and cold water and whisk well. This will keep it from clumping when it's added to the hot broth. When the broth reaches a boil, stir in the cornmeal mixture. If you are using a salty chicken base, don't add more salt. Otherwise, add ¾ teaspoon. Lower the heat and simmer, stirring often for 20 to 30 minutes, until the cornmeal mush is smooth and very thick. (A spoon should almost be able to stand upright in it.) Be sure to scrape the bottom as you stir to prevent scorching.

4. Preheat the oven to 375°F. Lightly oil a 4-quart cazuela or other ovenproof casserole with a nonstick cooking spray. Pour half the mush into the cazuela, and then alternately layer the meat mixture and the olives. When both are used up, top with half of the grated cheese and then the remaining cornmeal mush. Bake approximately 1½ hours. Do not underbake, or the mush will not cook through. (It will still taste great, but it won't look very good.)

5. Remove from the oven and top with the remaining cheese. You may garnish the pie with wheel designs made of strips of red and green pepper, avocado slices, and toasted pine nuts or walnuts. These will sink into the cheese as the cheese melts. Return to the oven for 15 minutes more, allowing the cheese to brown a bit. Sprinkle with parsley or cilantro.

Washtunkala Cast-Iron Kettle Stew

As I write about on page 142, *washtunkala* is the Sioux word for a stew made with dried meat and cornmeal. Our version at The Fort uses fresh meat and corn, and we enrich the broth with a buffalo demi-glace to ensure a rich-tasting gravy. Outstanding.

SERVES 4–6

Ingredients

1½–2 pounds buffalo or beef tenderloin tips, cut into 1½-inch cubes

3–4 tablespoons olive oil

Salt and freshly ground pepper, to taste

¼ cup fresh thyme sprigs

1 (12-ounce) package frozen pearl onions

1 (12-ounce) package frozen corn

1½ cups chopped mild green chiles

4 cups rich buffalo stock or beef broth

½ cup hulled sunflower seeds, roasted

Directions

1. Pat the buffalo cubes dry with paper towels.

2. In a large sauté pan, over high heat, brown the buffalo in oil, making sure not to crowd the pan. Sprinkle the browned meat with salt and pepper and add the thyme. Add the onions, corn, and chiles. Sauté for 1 minute. Add buffalo stock and sunflower seeds.

3. Reduce the heat to low and simmer for 8 to 10 minutes, until the broth is slightly thickened. At the restaurant, we serve the stew in individual cast-iron kettles, with Fort-Style Potatoes with Corn and Anasazi Beans (page 117) on the side.

Toothless Charlie's Ground Buffalo or Beef Steak

Ground buffalo or ground sirloin makes delicious burgers, and this one is about as good as it gets. We named it after our friend Chief Big Cloud, also known as Charlie Randall; his poor teeth prevented him from chewing steak, but he happily could eat this. We add the vanilla and ice as "secret ingredients" to provide the desirable moisture.

SERVES 6

Ingredients

6 (8-ounce) beef or buffalo tenderloins, chopped into ¼-inch pieces

½ cup finely minced white onion or Bermuda onion

2 tablespoons Worcestershire sauce

1½–2 teaspoons seasoned salt

1 teaspoon pure vanilla extract

1½ cups finely crushed ice

Salt and freshly ground black pepper, to taste

Toasted walnut halves, for topping (optional)

1 large bunch whole Italian parsley leaves, for serving

Directions

1. Heat a skillet or charcoal grill to high heat. Combine meat, onion, Worcestershire, seasoned salt, vanilla, and ice in a mixing bowl. Divide the mixture into 6 equal portions and form patties approximately 1 inch thick. Be careful not to compress the meat too much. For medium-rare burgers with a well-done outer crust, wait until your grill or skillet is really hot before putting the meat on.

2. Cook the patties for 3 minutes per side for buffalo or 4 ½ minutes per side for beef. Season with salt and pepper while grilling and try to turn only once. If using buffalo, watch carefully, as the meat is lean and easy to overcook.

3. If Uncle Charlie is indeed toothless, then don't add nuts. But I enjoy these steaks best topped with toasted walnut halves, or "eagles," and placed on a bed of parsley.

Mountains Meet the Sea—Buffalo Sirloin with Marinated Grilled Shrimp

A surf and turf special, this combination is the best of both worlds! One of The Fort's most popular entrées.

Ingredients

1 cup olive oil

¼ cup chopped parsley

2 tablespoons lemon juice

3 tablespoons Frank's RedHot Wing Sauce

2 tablespoons minced garlic

2 tablespoons tomato paste

2 teaspoons oregano

1 teaspoon salt

1 teaspoon black pepper

2 pounds shrimp (U/12 or U/15)

4 (5- or 6-ounce) buffalo sirloin or tenderloin steaks

Directions

1. Mix all ingredients from olive oil through black pepper and marinate the shrimp in this mixture for 2 hours. Then thread the shrimp on skewers.

2. Prepare the steaks and grill them as described in the recipe for Uncle Dick's "Incorrect" Buffalo or Beef Steak (page 146, minus the toppings).

3. When the steaks are 3 to 5 minutes from being done, throw the shrimp skewers on the grill and cook them just until they are no longer translucent; the meat will turn white and then pink. Do not overcook the shrimp! You want them tender and juicy.

Poultry, Pork, and Lamb

William Bent's Teriyaki Quail

Since much of the West was built by Asians, many of whom were from Japan, it's not surprising that teriyaki sauce would find its way into the cooking pretty early in the game. John Jacob Astor hired Hawaiians to work as Northwest trappers, and these folks took to teriyaki as well. We serve more than 1,000 quails a week at The Fort, so I figure we must be doing something right! We partially bone the little birds by removing the rib cages and serve them with the legs, thighs, and wings attached to the breast meat. Two or three quails make a fantastic dish.

SERVES 4

Ingredients

1 cup soy sauce

1 cup orange juice

1 cup water

½ cup mirin (rice wine) or dry sherry

¼ cup sugar

¼ cup finely chopped orange peel

2 tablespoons minced fresh ginger

3 cloves garlic, finely minced or smashed

2 whole star anise

8 (2½- to 3½-ounce) partially boned quail

8 orange slices, for garnish

Directions

1. In a saucepan, combine soy sauce, orange juice, water, rice wine, sugar, orange peel, ginger, garlic, and star anise and bring to a boil over high heat. Lower the heat and simmer for 5 minutes. Let cool.

2. Place the quail in a single layer in a pan, pour the marinade over, and let the quail marinate for 2 to 4 hours. Do not leave the birds in the marinade for longer than 8 hours or they will become unpalatably salty.

3. When ready to cook the quail, heat the grill to medium or preheat the broiler. Cook the quail for 3 to 5 minutes on each side or until cooked through. Garnish each bird with an orange slice.

Quail en Quinoa

My father became enamored with quinoa when he first traveled to Peru. It's cultivated high in the Andes and does well in our Rocky Mountains, too. A mild-tasting grain packed with nutrition, when it is paired with quail, its nuttiness and soft texture absorb the bird's juices for a delectable dish. This is essentially a one-dish meal, and a great addition to a buffet, hot or cold.

SERVES 4–6

Ingredients

3 tablespoons unsalted butter

3 tablespoons olive or canola oil

4–6 partially boned quail

2 cups quinoa

4–6 Portuguese linguica sausages

1½ cups chopped yellow onion (1 large)

2 cups chopped mild green chiles (two 7-ounce cans)

½ cup pitted ripe black olives

6 cups chicken broth

½ cup walnut halves, lightly toasted, for garnish

Directions

1. Preheat the oven to 325°F. Place the butter and oil in a large sauté pan or skillet over medium-high heat. When butter begins to turn clear, add the quail, in small batches, and brown on both sides, 6 to 8 minutes. Remove the quail to a cutting board and cut into quarters.

2. Butter a 3- to 4-quart baking dish or casserole.

3. In a sieve, carefully rinse the quinoa in cold or lukewarm running water to remove any bitter residue. Place half of the quinoa in the prepared baking dish, spreading it into an even layer.

4. Cut the linguica sausages into bite-size pieces and arrange them on top of the quinoa. Add the quail pieces, onion, green chiles, and olives. Cover with the remaining quinoa and add the chicken broth. Cover tightly with aluminum foil and bake for 60 to 80 minutes, until quinoa is fluffy and most of the liquid has been absorbed. Garnish the casserole with walnuts just before serving.

Charbroiled Quail with Red Chile Honey

My dad told me how honeybees were imported to our continent by European settlers and quickly adapted to every climate and region. Early settlers relied on honey to sweeten just about everything because cane sugar from the Caribbean was expensive and in short supply. Native Americans viewed the insects as harbingers of encroaching change: when they saw bees, they knew white men were about 50 miles away. On the other hand, quail are indigenous to North America and were commonly hunted, along with grouse and prairie chickens, by trappers, settlers, soldiers, and Indians. When red meat was scarce, upland game was a good substitute.

SERVES 4

Ingredients

1 rounded tablespoon pure ground New Mexican red chile (Dixon preferred)

1 cup honey

8 partially boned quail (see Note)

8 tbs canola oil (1 tbs per quail)

Directions

1. In a small saucepan, stir the chile in the honey, over low heat to a simmer for 10 minutes to combine their flavors.

2. Fire up the grill, either electric or charcoal, to medium high heat. Brush the quail with the oil, and charbroil them over indirect heat section on the grill, (usually on the side of the grill), for 3 to 5 minutes per side. Brush both sides of the birds with the chile honey when they are nearly cooked. If you glaze them too soon, the honey will burn and you will end up with charred quail.

3. After placing the quail on serving plates, brush them once more with glaze.

Note: If you use quail that are not partially boned, allow 5 to 8 minutes per side of cooking time.

Applewood Smoked Duck Breast

Our former executive chef Dave Woolley developed this recipe when my dad and I craved crispy *maigre de canard*, reminiscent of the duck we had tasted in France. The duck has a layer of fat on top of the breast that is broiled until crispy, and the breast meat tastes delicately smoky. I think this is best served on a bed of sautéed spinach with a side of Cha Cha Murphys (page 115).

SERVES 2–4

Ingredients

3 tablespoons hot water

1 tablespoon brown sugar

1 tablespoon kosher salt

2 (6-ounce) boneless duck breast fillets

1 applewood or hickory aluminum foil smoking bag

Directions

1. Mix the water, brown sugar, and salt until the salt and sugar are dissolved to make a brine. Place duck fillets in a shallow pan, and add brine and enough cold water to cover them. Cover the pan and let it sit overnight in refrigerator.

2. Preheat the oven to 250°F.

3. Remove fillets from the brine and place them in a smoking bag. Fold the end of the bag to seal it. Place the bag on the middle rack of the oven and smoke 35 minutes for rare, 40 minutes for medium, and 45 minutes for well done. Outside the oven, let the duck rest in the bag for 5 to 10 minutes.

4. Open the bag carefully to avoid being burned by hot steam. Remove the skin from the fillets and discard it. Slice the breasts and serve.

Balsamic Fig Duck

Former executive chef Ian Stewart-Shefalo created this delicious duck breast presentation in 2015, and it has been a guest favorite since! The combination of figs and balsamic vinegar pairs beautifully with duck.

SERVES 4

Ingredients

8 duck breasts

¼ cup puréed onion (use blender)

1 cup fig spread

2 tablespoons balsamic vinegar

⅛ teaspoon ground clove

½ cup hot water

¼ cup honey

½ cup chicken stock

Salt and pepper, to taste

Directions

1. Preheat the oven to 425°F.

2. Spray a cast iron oven-proof pan with canola oil. Heat the oiled pan, over high heat on the stove. Sear the duck breasts skin side down, until medium brown, for 2-3 minutes; flip and sear the meat side for another 2-3 minutes. Return the duck to skin side down and then place the cast iron pan in the oven and cook for 10 to 12 minutes.

3. While the duck is in the oven, combine all other ingredients to make the sauce on the stove in a small saucepan. Heat all ingredients on medium heat, while stirring frequently for 3-5 minutes, until it comes to a simmer. Lower the heat and continue to simmer on low heat until the sauce is fully incorporated and thickened. Turn the heat down to warm.

4. Serve with warm fig sauce drizzled over the duck breasts.

Cha Cha Chicken

Our first restaurant manager, Luis Bonachea, joined us when we opened in 1963 and brought with him culinary influences from his native Cuba. This chicken is typical of the sort of dishes cooked in that Caribbean nation, with a sweet fruitiness that caramelizes on the meat during cooking to give it a superb *agridulce*, or sweet-and-sour, flavor. If you want to use small chicken legs (called drumettes) or wings, prepare them in advance and serve them as a party appetizer. Delicious!

SERVES 4-6

Ingredients

MARINADE

2 cups orange juice without pulp

¼ cup soy sauce

5 tablespoons honey

4 tablespoons fresh lime juice

3 tablespoons unsalted butter, melted

2 tablespoons chopped Italian parsley

2 tablespoons chopped fresh cilantro

2 tablespoons dry mustard

2 tablespoons finely minced, peeled fresh ginger

½ teaspoon cayenne pepper

2 cloves garlic, peeled and minced

HENS

2–3 Cornish hens, cut in half; or 4–6 bone-in split chicken breasts; or 4–6 whole chicken legs (drumstick and thigh)

1 orange, thinly sliced

1 lime, thinly sliced

1 tablespoon canola oil

Dash of salt

Cayenne, to taste

Fresh mint sprigs, for garnish

1 recipe Rice Pilaf (page 120)

Directions

1. In a food processor or blender, combine all of the marinade ingredients. Pulse on and off until well blended.

2. Place the chicken in a glass bowl and add the marinade. On top of the marinaded chicken, also add the orange and lime slices. Cover the bowl and place in the refrigerator. The chicken needs only a few hours to marinate; however, longer is better and overnight is dandy.

3. When you're ready to cook the chicken, preheat the oven to 325°F. Remove chicken from the marinade and place it on a shallow baking pan completely lined with aluminum foil that has been coated with oil. Parchment paper also works, but cut it large enough to extend all the way up the sides of the pan to prevent the syrup from leaking beneath it. Sprinkle the chicken with salt and cayenne and bake for 35 minutes, then raise the heat to broil and cook another 10 minutes, until the skin is nice and crispy.

4. Garnish with the mint sprigs. Serve chicken on a bed of pilaf.

Baked Stuffed Pumpkin

This recipe, which was served at The Fort in the early 1960s, is one of my personal favorites, and because it's served in a pumpkin, it's a natural for Halloween. When we decided to write this book, I invited my editorial team to dinner on a cool fall evening and served the stew. We dug in and got even more excited about the book! Native Americans prepare something very similar, which makes sense, as pumpkin is a squash and thus one of three sacred sisters. Native peoples also use a lot of toasted sunflower seeds, which gives this stew a distinctive flavor. Bring out your favorite hot sauce to serve with this comforting autumn dish.

SERVES 6–8

Ingredients

1 (4- to 5-pound) sugar pumpkin

2 tablespoons unsalted butter, melted

Fine sea salt, to taste

Coarsely ground black pepper, to taste

2 tablespoons olive oil

2 cups chopped white onion (1 large)

1 pound ground buffalo or lean ground beef

2 cups fresh corn kernels or 1 (11-ounce) can white shoepeg corn, drained

2 cups fresh green beans

1 cup chopped green bell pepper

1 cup diced, cooked chicken

1 cup hulled sunflower seeds

4 cups chicken broth

2 fresh peaches, peeled, pitted, and sliced

Hot pepper sauce (optional)

Directions

1. Preheat the oven to 350°F.

2. With a large, sharp knife, cut the top off the pumpkin, jack-o-lantern style. With a large spoon, scrape out the seeds and strings (save the seeds to salt and bake for a snack). Rub the inside of the pumpkin generously with melted butter, and season it with salt and pepper. Place the pumpkin in a roasting pan. Bake, with the top off, for about 45 minutes or until the pumpkin is tender but still holds its shape. Check after 30 minutes for liquid buildup. Using a long-handled ladle, remove any juice and discard it. The pumpkin may collapse while baking if you don't remove the liquid.

3. Meanwhile, in a Dutch oven or heavy-bottomed sauté pan, heat the olive oil. Add onion and cook over medium heat until translucent, about 5 minutes. Add buffalo or beef and sauté until browned, 6 to 8 minutes. Stir in corn, green beans, bell pepper, diced chicken, sunflower seeds, chicken broth, and peaches. When the liquid comes to a boil, reduce heat to low and simmer the stew gently for about 40 minutes to blend the flavors.

4. Carefully lift the baked pumpkin onto a round serving platter. Ladle stew into the pumpkin and top with the lid. As you serve, be sure to scrape the inside of the pumpkin to mix some of its delicious flesh into the stew.

Baked Chicken Adobe

This is one of our most popular entrées, conceived by our former sous chef, Juan Zepeda. Juan told me he came up with the idea to tempt his children and divert their attraction to fast food. He relied on his Mexican heritage to make the chicken taste as it does—and it's a winner!

SERVES 4

Ingredients

4 (8- to 10-ounce) whole boneless, skinless chicken breasts

6 ounces Monterey Jack cheese, cut into 4 (1½ x ½-inch) sticks

4 (¼-inch-thick) slices of ham

1½ cups finely ground tortilla chips

½ cup breadcrumbs

¾ cup all-purpose flour

Salt and freshly ground pepper, to taste

1–1½ cups milk

Canola oil, enough to fill a medium skillet ½ inch deep

Directions

The first step can be done the day before, as it requires freezing the bundles of chicken 3 hours or overnight.

1. Lightly pound the chicken breasts between sheets of plastic wrap to flatten. If one is particularly thick, you may want to butterfly it. Wrap each cheese stick in a slice of ham. Place a ham-and-cheese bundle on the rougher-textured cut side of each chicken breast, folding the short ends of the chicken up over the ham. Fold in the long sides of the breast to completely enclose the bundle. Place the breasts seam side down in a pan with the smooth side up, cover and freeze for at least three hours, or overnight. This step can also be done the day before.

2. Preheat the oven to 350°F.

3. Combine ground tortilla chips and breadcrumbs on a plate. This should be enough breading, but if you are using very large chicken breasts, you may need more. On a separate plate, combine flour, salt, and pepper. Place milk in a wide-mouthed shallow bowl.

4. Dip the frozen chicken breasts first in flour and then in milk. Dredge the chicken in the crumbs, pressing firmly so that the breading adheres.

5. Place the skillet of oil over high heat. Fry the chicken breasts, one at a time, in hot oil, turning with tongs to brown them on all sides. Place the browned chicken on paper towels to drain excess oil, then arrange on a baking sheet. Bake for 20 to 30 minutes, until cooked through. This technique allows the chicken to cook evenly and thoroughly with minimal frying.

Country Captain Chicken

When my mother and father opened The Fort in 1963, I was still a girl but eagerly tucked into the food served in the restaurant. This was one of my favorites back then, and it still holds up all these years later. I attribute its place on our menu to my mom, who was from the South, where the mild chicken curry dish originated. The story goes that curry was introduced to the lowlands of South Carolina, where rice was a significant crop, by a sea captain who had sailed to India sometime in the 1700s. We adapted this recipe from one in the *American Heritage Cookbook*, and while it has a long list of ingredients, don't let that scare you. It's quick and simple to put together and oh so good!

SERVES 4–6

Ingredients

½ cup all-purpose flour

1 teaspoon salt

¼ teaspoon freshly ground pepper

3 pounds skinless, bone-in chicken parts

4–6 tablespoons unsalted butter

½ cup finely chopped yellow onion

½ cup finely chopped green bell pepper

1 large clove garlic, peeled and minced

1½–2 teaspoons curry powder, to taste

2–3 curry bush leaves (optional) (see Note)

½ teaspoon dried thyme

1 (14½-ounce) can stewed tomatoes

3 tablespoons dried currants

4 cups cooked white rice

½ cup blanched sliced almonds, lightly toasted, for garnish

Mango chutney, for serving

Directions

1. Combine flour, salt, and pepper on a plate.

2. Pat the chicken pieces dry with paper towels and coat with the seasoned flour.

3. Place 4 tablespoons of butter in a large sauté pan or skillet over medium heat. When the butter turns clear, add the chicken. Reduce heat to medium–low, and cook for 10 to 12 minutes, until the chicken is well browned on both sides. If all the fat is absorbed before the chicken browns, add the remaining butter. Remove the chicken and set aside.

4. Add the onion, bell pepper, garlic, curry powder, curry bush leaves, and thyme to the skillet and cook for a few minutes over low heat, stirring in all the brown particles. Add the tomatoes and chicken, cover, and simmer for 20 to 30 minutes, until tender.

5. Just before serving, stir in the currants. Serve the chicken over hot, fluffy white rice. Garnish with toasted almonds and serve the chutney on the side.

Note: Curry bush leaves are sold in Asian markets. You can also order them online. See "Where to Find It!"

Thanksgiving Turkey with Piñon Nut Stuffing

We started making this stuffing for The Fort's Thanksgiving turkeys in the 1960s, at which time we smoked whole birds outside in a large smokehouse. The aroma of smoking poultry wafted over the valley and attracted bears to our property. Try as they might, they could not get into the smokehouse, which was securely locked. I used to joke that these large marauders were suitors for my pet bear, Sissy, but I knew even then that they were more interested in the turkeys than in Sissy. When we ventured from The Fort's walls, we had to bang metal pans together to scare away the bears! My son, Oren, makes this stuffing for his family every Thanksgiving.

SERVES 6–8

Ingredients

STUFFING

½ pound chestnuts, either fresh roasted, peeled, and chopped or dry roasted from a jar

8 tablespoons (1 stick) unsalted butter

1 clove garlic, peeled and minced

2 cups stale bread cubes

⅔ cup chicken broth

2 tablespoons dry sherry

½ cup heavy cream

½ cup chopped green chiles, canned or fresh

2 shallots, peeled and minced

2 celery stalks, diced

½ cup chopped Italian parsley

¼ cup whole cilantro leaves

2–3 teaspoons freshly ground black pepper, to taste

1 teaspoon chopped fresh rosemary

1 teaspoon salt

2 pinches fresh thyme leaf or 1 pinch dry

½ cup pine nuts, toasted

TURKEY

16 tablespoons (2 sticks) unsalted butter

⅛ cup salt (for a 15-pound turkey)

¼ cup freshly ground black pepper (for a 15-pound turkey)

1 cup dry white wine

3 tablespoons fresh rosemary or 1 tablespoon dry, divided

1. To roast the chestnuts, cut an X on the flat side of each nut. Place the nuts in a dry cast-iron skillet and toast over medium-high heat, shaking the pan often, until the shells start browning and the edges of the X begin to pull away from the nuts. Parts of them will be quite dark, and they will smell wonderful! Chestnuts peel more easily when they're warm. Use a sharp paring knife to peel back both the outer shell and the inner membrane. The inner membrane can be quite stubborn, but the result justifies the effort.

2. For the stuffing: Melt the butter in a sauté pan over medium-low heat and cook the garlic until golden. Add the bread cubes and stir constantly over medium heat, until golden. Remove the bread with a slotted spoon and set aside. In the same pan, combine the chicken broth, sherry, cream, chiles, shallots, celery, parsley, cilantro, pepper, rosemary, salt, and thyme. Simmer for 2 minutes, over medium heat, to release the flavors. Add the bread cube mixture, chestnuts, and pine nuts. Mix well, cover, and bring to room temperature before using to stuff the bird.

3. To prepare the turkey: Melt the butter and stir in the salt and pepper. Rub the turkey with the butter mixture inside and out. Use the remaining butter to make the basting sauce. Combine the butter with the wine and one-third of the rosemary in a small saucepan. Boil for 2 minutes on high heat, then remove from the heat and use to baste the turkey every 15 minutes while roasting.

4. Preheat the oven to 375°F.

5. Fill both cavities of the bird with the stuffing. Sew up with a trussing cord and bind the wings and drumsticks tight alongside the bird's body. Sprinkle the remaining rosemary over the bird.

ROCKY MOUNTAIN PINE NUTS

Pine nuts from New Mexico and Colorado are called *piñones* (peen-YO-nays) or *piñons*. In Italy they are called *pignoli* or *pignolia*. Actually seeds from pine trees, the small, elongated nuts are found nestled in the large cones. For centuries they have been gathered in the wintertime in our neck of the woods, first by Native Americans and then by settlers in our mountains. After the first snowfall, it's easy to follow the tracks of ground squirrels to their burrows, where several gallons of nuts can be dug up and toted away. Most folks leave enough for the squirrels so that they don't starve—and live to lead us to their burrows next year.

Everyone roasts the nuts to accentuate their sweet flavor. I love them in salads, stuffing, and sauces. The Indians still crack them between their teeth and skillfully extract the meat with their tongues. Today, it's common in Santa Fe (and other cities') movie theaters to find a carpet of empty pine nut shells on the floor after the lights go up.

6. Reduce the oven temperature to 325°F.

7. Place the turkey on a rack in a shallow roasting pan. Do not add water. Cover the turkey with a loose tent of aluminum foil and roast for 15 minutes per pound plus 1 hour for the stuffing.

8. Remove the foil 30 minutes before roasting is done. Test for doneness with a reliable meat thermometer; this is the only way to be sure it is done. The final temperature for safety and doneness is 180°F in the thigh and at least 165°F in the breast and stuffing. The juices should run clear, not pink. Test the temperature early and often. An overcooked turkey is dry, tough, and pasty in texture.

Variation: Hickory Smokey Turkey. You can also use a covered barbecue or smoke roaster to cook the turkey over indirect heat and use damp hickory chips on the fire for a smoke flavor. Don't overdo the amount or length of smoke—15 minutes of smoke is enough. Roast the bird until a meat thermometer registers 180°F in the thigh and at least 165°F in the breast and stuffing, usually about 4 hours. A pan of water in the cooker, under the bird, helps to keep it moist.

Note: You may make the stuffing a day ahead of time and refrigerate it overnight, but warm it slightly before you stuff the bird. Bringing the stuffing to room temperature before filling the bird is necessary to allow the stuffing to cook all the way through. Be sure to remove all stuffing from the carcass after dining and store in a separate bowl.

Santa Fe Pork Adobada

In Santa Fe more pork is eaten during the winter holidays than any other meat or poultry. The tradition harkens back to the very early days of the city, which was established by the Spanish in 1610. The Europeans had claimed the region as the Kingdom of New Mexico in 1540 and set up the capital in San Juan Pueblo in 1548—about 25 miles north of Santa Fe. Don Pedro de Peralta moved the capital to Santa Fe in 1610, where it remains to this day. As well as organizing their own style of government, the Spaniards introduced domesticated animals to the area: pigs, sheep, cattle, chickens, and horses. For economic reasons, the locals ate more pork, poultry, and mutton than they did beef. During Christmas, modern-day residents still prepare pork posole, pork-filled tamales, barbecued pork ribs, and deep-fried crispy pork pieces called carnitas. Pork Adobada is a popular dish as well, with warm, deep flavors that pop from the chile marinade. We served it at The Fort in the 1960s—and still love it today.

SERVES 4-6

Ingredients

1 cup chicken broth

½ cup medium red chile caribe (coarsely ground chile)

½ teaspoon dried Mexican oregano

½ teaspoon salt

4-6 (7-ounce) lean pork rib chops, thickly cut

4 cups cooked white rice or mashed potatoes

Directions

1. In a shallow baking dish large enough to hold the chops, combine chicken broth, chile, oregano, and salt. Dredge the chops in the marinade to coat well. Place the chops in the marinade, cover, and refrigerate for at least 4 hours. They are even better when marinated for 8 hours!

2. Preheat the oven to 350°F.

3. Transfer the chops and marinade to a foil-lined pan and bake, covered tightly with aluminum foil, for 35 minutes. Remove the foil, baste with pan juices, and continue to bake for 10 minutes. If juices evaporate and the chile threatens to burn, replace the foil for the last few minutes. Serve the chops over hot, fluffy rice or mashed potatoes.

Dixon and Ancho Chile Rub Pork Tenderloin

Pork tenderloin is a great choice for a dinner party or family gathering. It takes on the flavors of a rub or marinade as readily as does chicken and cooks in a short time without losing any of its natural moisture. Our former executive chef Geoffrey Groditsky came up with this dry chile rub for pork, made with Dixon red chile powder and dried ancho chiles, which have a degree of sweetness. We like to serve it with Rice Pilaf (page 120) and Zuni Succotash with Toasted Sunflower Seed Hearts (page 111).

SERVES 4-6

Ingredients

CHILE RUB

½ yellow onion

¼ cup garlic cloves, roasted and peeled

1 tablespoon New Mexican ground red chile (Dixon preferred)

1 teaspoon ground ancho chile

1 teaspoon ground cumin

¼ cup canola oil

¼ cup Thai sweet red chili sauce

2 tablespoons cider vinegar

Salt and freshly ground pepper, to taste

PORK TENDERLOIN

2-3 (1-pound) pork tenderloins, trimmed

2-3 tablespoons olive or canola oil

VEGETABLES

2 tablespoons unsalted butter

1 cup fire-roasted corn

1 cup chopped mild green chiles, fresh or canned

1 small red onion, peeled and thinly sliced

1 cup diced zucchini

Salt and freshly ground pepper, to taste

CHIPOTLE SAUCE

2 teaspoons olive or canola oil

2 chipotle chiles en adobo (canned), minced

1 cup heavy cream

2 tablespoons dry white wine

Salt and freshly ground pepper, to taste

2-3 cups hot cooked wild rice

Directions

1. To make the rub: In a food processor, combine onion, garlic, ground chiles, cumin, oil, sweet chili sauce, and vinegar. Pulse on and off until almost puréed. Taste and season with salt and pepper.

2. Rub the tenderloins with the seasoning mixture. Cover and marinate, refrigerated overnight.

3. Preheat the oven to 400°F.

4. To make the tenderloin: Place oil in a large sauté pan or skillet over medium-high heat. Sear the tenderloins, turning with tongs to brown them on all sides. Remove the seared tenderloins to a shallow roasting pan. Roast on the middle rack of the oven for 15 to 20 minutes, until pork is medium to medium-well done. Allow tenderloins to rest for 5 minutes, then slice on the bias.

5. To make the vegetables: In a sauté pan over medium heat, melt butter. Add the corn, green chile, onion, and zucchini and sauté for 3 to 5 minutes, until tender crisp. Season to taste with salt and pepper.

6. To make the sauce: Sauté chipotle in olive oil, over medium-high heat, for 1 minute. Add the cream and wine and cook, stirring, until the sauce is reduced to about ¾ cup.

7. Serve the sliced tenderloins with wild rice and sautéed vegetables. Drizzle each serving with the chipotle sauce.

Antonio Archuleta's Red Chile–Blue Corn Enchiladas

Taos native Antonio, who made The Fort's furniture for over 40 years, shared his family's enchilada recipe with me—and now I am honored to share it with you. He passed away several years ago, but his presence is always with us at The Fort. When you make these enchiladas, you will "enjoy a very special New Mexican dish," as Antonio said.

SERVES 6

Ingredients

PORK

1 (2½-pound) boneless pork roast

1 onion, peeled and quartered

5–6 cloves garlic, peeled and crushed with flat side of chef's knife

2 teaspoons salt

RED CHILE SAUCE

3 tablespoons canola oil

3 tablespoons all-purpose flour

3 tablespoons medium to hot ground red New Mexican chile

1 clove garlic, peeled and minced

ENCHILADA ASSEMBLY

12 blue, yellow, or white corn tortillas

3–5 tablespoons canola oil

4 cups shredded cheddar cheese (longhorn sharp cheddar preferred)

1 small yellow onion, peeled and finely chopped

2–3 ripe plum tomatoes, diced, for garnish

2–3 cups shredded iceberg lettuce, for garnish

Directions

1. To make the pork: Cut the roast into 2-inch pieces and place in a Dutch oven with enough water to cover by 2 inches. Add onion, garlic, salt, and oregano. Bring to a boil over medium-high heat. Skim off and discard foam that rises to the top. Reduce heat to low and simmer gently for about 1 hour, until very tender. Remove the pork with a slotted spoon and set aside. Boil down the meat broth to about 5 cups and reserve for the chile sauce. When cool enough to handle, shred the pork into small pieces, and remove and discard excess fat. Strain the broth and discard onion and garlic. Reserve the broth for sauce.

2. To make the chile sauce: In a large, deep sauté pan or skillet, combine oil and flour. Cook, stirring, over medium heat for 2 to 3 minutes, until the flour turns golden brown. Remove from heat and stir

in the ground red chile. Mix well, then add the pork broth. Mix well again and add the minced garlic. Simmer the sauce over low heat for 20 minutes, stirring often. The sauce should thicken and be reduced to about 4 cups.

3. Preheat the oven to 375°F.

4. To assemble the enchiladas: Lightly oil a large oven-proof platter or large, shallow baking dish. In a saucepan, combine shredded pork and 1½ cups of the chile sauce. Heat, stirring, until the mixture comes to a simmer, then set aside. In a separate skillet, heat the oil. With tongs dip a tortilla in the hot oil to soften, then dip it in the chile sauce. Arrange 6 dipped tortillas on the platter, overlapping slightly. Sprinkle about one-third of the cheese over the tortillas, then sprinkle with half of the chopped onion. Top with half of the shredded pork and a little extra chile sauce. Add another layer of tortillas, cheese, onion, pork, and chile sauce. Top with remaining cheese. Bake the enchiladas for 10 minutes, until hot and bubbling. Remove and garnish with diced tomatoes and shredded lettuce.

Crispy Southwestern Pork Shank
with Chipotle BBQ Sauce

My dad, who was born in Pennsylvania and influenced by German cooking during his childhood, was so fond of *schweine haux* (swine hocks) that we put our version on the menu in 1999. Our customers were delighted with these deep-fried shanks (in place of hocks). One evening my husband, Jeremy, was drafted to help out in the restaurant kitchen, and after submerging one pork shank after another in sizzling fat and seeing the skin crisp and the meat nearly fall off the bone, he dreamed of nothing else but eating them. We dined at The Fort the next night expressly to satisfy Jeremy's hunger! You will probably have to ask the butcher to order pork shanks. Allow 1 shank per serving, and expect each one to weigh from 16 to 18 ounces.

SERVES 4–6

Ingredients

4–6 pork shanks

1 large onion, quartered

4 carrots, peeled and quartered

4 celery stalks, cut into 2- to 3-inch lengths

8 cups chicken broth or water, for braising

4–6 cloves garlic, crushed

1 teaspoon salt

½ teaspoon freshly ground black pepper

Canola oil for deep-frying

2–3 tablespoons unsalted butter

16 ounces fresh baby spinach

½ cup caramelized onions

1 cup buffalo stock, veal stock, or reduced-sodium beef or chicken broth

1 recipe Bay's Georgia Green Chile Grits (page 108)

1 cup Chipotle BBQ Sauce (page 67)

Directions

1. In a large Dutch oven, put the shanks, onion, carrots, and celery and add 8 cups water or chicken stock to cover. Toss in the garlic and season with the salt and pepper. Cover the pot and bring to a boil over high heat. When the liquid boils, reduce the heat to low and braise for about 1½ hours, checking occasionally. The pork should be tender when done, but not quite falling off the bone. Remove the shanks and let them cool before going on to the next step.

2. Preheat the oven to 400°F and a deep fryer to 325°F.

3. Carefully lower the pork shanks, one at a time, into the fryer and cook for 5 minutes each. Drain the shanks on paper towels, then transfer them to a baking sheet. Roast in the oven for about 10 minutes to ensure that the shanks heat all the way through.

4. Meanwhile, in a large sauté pan, over medium heat, melt the butter. Add the spinach and onions and sauté for 2 to 3 minutes, until slightly wilted. Add the stock and cook over medium-high heat, stirring, until liquid is reduced by half. Place grits and spinach in individual serving bowls and place a cooked shank on top. Drizzle with Chipotle BBQ Sauce.

General Armijo's Grilled Lamb Chops

As my dad explained it, General Manuel Armijo was the last governor of New Mexico while it was still under Mexican rule, and it's no coincidence that he governed at the end of an era. He was not well liked, and when it became apparent that Mexico had no money to wage battle against General Stephen W. Kearny's army during the Mexican-American War, he took a bribe and skedaddled. Detractors claimed that he'd also been a sheep thief, stealing sheep and then selling them back to the original owners. Our lamb chops are named for this notorious scoundrel. Serve them with Red Chile Sauce (page 60) or mango chutney.

SERVES 6

Ingredients

4½ teaspoons medium ground black pepper

3 teaspoons fine sea salt

¾ teaspoon lemon crystals (citric acid or sour salt)

6 (¾- to 1-pound) double rib or loin lamb chops, trimmed of fat

6 tbs canola oil (1 tbs oil per chop)

1 recipe Red Chile Sauce (page 60)

Directions

1. Preheat the oven to broil or heat a grill to high. Combine the pepper, sea salt, and lemon crystals, and rub each chop with the mixture, then brush with oil. Place the chops about 6 inches from the heat source.

2. The grilling time will depend on the thickness of the chops. For a chop that's a nice juicy, pink, medium-rare on the inside and wonderfully charred on the outside, about 7 minutes per side will do. Before turning, swab the tops with oil. Serve with Red Chile Sauce on the side.

Note: While you can find a lot of New Zealand lamb, it's usually too young to have much taste. I prefer hogget or yearling lamb because the meat is much more flavorful. If you cannot find a butcher to cut double chops, buy the thickest rib or loin chops you can find. If you are preparing this dish for many people, butterflied leg of lamb works very nicely and is a little less expensive. Because the meat is not of uniform thickness, there will be medium-rare to well-done pieces to satisfy the varied palates of your guests.

Herbed Lamb Chops

Double lamb chops are tender and sweet and so good that they are always an indulgence. These are cut from racks of lamb and therefore are sometimes called rib chops. Cut through the racks so that each chop has two long bones, with the meat scraped away to make them frenched. These are divine rubbed gently with garlic and fresh herbs.

SERVES 4–6

Ingredients

6-8 cloves garlic, peeled

½ cup Italian parsley

½ cup fresh mint leaves

4 sprigs fresh rosemary

Salt and freshly ground pepper, to taste

2 racks of lamb, frenched and cut into double chops (2 bones each)

1 recipe Rice Pilaf (page 120)

Directions

1. In a food processor combine garlic, parsley, mint, rosemary, salt and pepper. Pulse on and off until finely chopped. Rub the lamb with the herb seasoning.

2. Preheat the oven to 400°F.

3. Place a large sauté pan or skillet over medium-high heat. Place lamb chops fat side down in the hot pan. With tongs, turn the chops to brown evenly on all sides. Remove lamb from sauté pan to a sheet pan and roast in the oven for 10 to 12 minutes for medium-rare to medium. Serve with rice pilaf.

Marinated Rack of Lamb with Couscous

At Bent's Fort, they traded spices, legumes, and indigo ink, all part of the Chinese, East India, and Portuguese spice trade from North Africa, India, and China. We feature this delicious Moroccan-style lamb dish as an homage to the international trade and tastes that were at Bent's Fort in the 1800s!

SERVES 4-6

Ingredients

Full Rack of Lamb-(8 ribs), cut into 1-2 rib portions.

1 cup Dijon mustard

1 spray (30 seconds) of canola oil for sauté pan

½ cup minced onion

3¾ cups chicken stock

2 cups pearl/Israeli couscous

¼ cup pine nuts, toasted

3 sprigs fresh garden mint leaves (remove stems)

4 tablespoons of chopped fresh mint as garnish for ribs

2 tablespoons olive oil

Harissa paste, as condiment

Directions

1. Place the lamb ribs in a non-reactive marinade pan (glass or ceramic). Rub the lamb ribs with Dijon mustard. Cover and place in the refrigerator to marinate for 2-4 hours, or overnight.

2. Preheat oven to 350 degrees

3. Spray a large sauté pan with canola oil, place on the stove over high heat, and sear the lamb ribs for 4-5 minutes per side in sauté pan. Remove from stove. Spray canola oil in a large 9" x 13" or larger baking pan. Place ribs in pan.

4. Cook the ribs in oven for 20 minutes, for medium rare, or 25 minutes for medium.

5. While the ribs are in the oven, prepare the couscous.

6. In a sauté pan over medium heat, lightly sauté onions in olive oil until translucent. Add chicken stock and bring to a boil. Once boiling, add couscous, pine nuts, and mint. Reduce heat and simmer pearled couscous, covered, for 10-15 minutes. Make sure it is fully cooked but still moist before serving.

7. Take the lamb ribs out of the oven place on top of the couscous on individual warmed plates (1-2 ribs per serving) or full rack-8 ribs on a platter to serve family style. Garnish with freshly chopped mint per plate (1 tbs) or platter (4 tbs).

8. Use Harissa paste as a condiment to accompany the lamb.

# Fish and Seafood

Taos Indian-Style Trout

When my father wrote about this traditional Native American dish, he explained that he had gotten the recipe from his friend Mary Schlosser, a full-blooded Taos Indian married to Carl Schlosser. The couple ran Carl's Trading Post for many years in Taos, New Mexico. "It sounds a bit odd but is excellent," Dad said. "The bacon with the mint leaves imparts a delicious herbal taste."

This trout was on our menu for many years but was removed in 1976 when we sold The Fort. My family bought back the restaurant in 1986. Although Dad wanted the dish back on the menu immediately, our chefs were not sure our patrons would embrace a dish that featured a trout with head and tail intact. Shortly after my father died, we honored his request and put the trout on the menu. Dad was right. Our guests love it! You will, too.

SERVES 1

Ingredients

1 (12- to 16-ounce) boneless, butterflied trout with head and tail attached

6 short sprigs fresh mint

1 teaspoon salt, plus more to taste2 tablespoons olive oil

Freshly ground black pepper

2 strips uncooked bacon

Lemon slices

Directions

1. Rinse the trout and pat dry with paper towels.

2. Combine the mint sprigs with the salt and olive oil and mash them to release their flavor. Fill the cavity of the trout with the oily leaves and season the outside with salt and pepper.

3. Wind a strip of bacon around the fish near the tail and pin it in place with a toothpick. Repeat the process with the second strip of bacon, but closer to the head of the fish. The trout may be covered and refrigerated until ready to broil.

3. Twenty minutes in advance of cooking, preheat the oven to broil. Place the fish on a broiling pan and cook 5 inches from the heat for about 5 to 7 minutes on each side, until the bacon is well crisped. Remove the toothpicks and serve the trout with lemon slices.

Owl Woman's Smoked Trout

We served this trout dish at The Fort in the 1960s. I found a description on a typed 1963 menu that was stapled to a colorfully woven Mexican mat. The dish is "named for William Bent's Cheyenne wife. The smoked fillets were prepared for us by Toklat in Ashcroft, Colorado, in the 60s. Sometimes large and sometimes small, the trout are boned, gently steamed to bring out the smoked flavor, and served with butter, chervil, and lemon sauce."

SERVES 4

Ingredients

4–6 six-ounce fillets smoked trout

4 tablespoons unsalted butter

Juice of 1 large lemon

1 teaspoon dried chervil

Directions

1. In a steamer pot, boil water and place the trout fillets in the steamer basket. Gently steam for 3 to 4 minutes or until warm.

2. Meanwhile, in a saucepan over low heat, melt the butter and add the lemon juice and chervil. Stir to combine, and pour over the trout fillets, which are delicious served with quinoa or wild rice.

Trout Stuffed with Corn, Piñones, and Green Chiles

Trout is in good supply in Colorado, where mountain streams and rivers offer them happy homes. We serve a lot of freshwater fish at The Fort, and this is one of our favorite recipes for special occasions. I first tasted this at the home of Priscilla Hoback, a renowned sculptor from Galisteo, New Mexico, and the daughter of my father's dear friend Rosalea Murphy. Priscilla is a marvelously creative cook, and although we had to adapt the recipe for the restaurant, it was inspired by her talent.

SERVES 6

Ingredients

1 cup fresh corn kernels (or canned or frozen)

¼ cup pine nuts, toasted

¾ cup chopped fresh medium-hot or mild green chiles

½ cup dried breadcrumbs

1 large egg

½ teaspoon dried dill weed

½ teaspoon dried thyme

Salt and freshly ground black pepper, to taste

6 (12-inch) rainbow or cutthroat trout, deboned and butterflied with head and tail still attached

3 tablespoons canola oil

Directions

1. Preheat the oven to 350°F.

2. Mix the corn with the pine nuts, chiles, and breadcrumbs. Beat the egg with the dill, thyme, and salt and pepper. Combine the corn and egg mixtures thoroughly and stuff into the cavity of each trout. Brush the fish with oil to coat. Bake for about 30 minutes.

SALMON: FRESH OR FROZEN?

In the late 1980s, my dad discovered the benefits of flash-frozen fish. At the same time, I owned a public relations company and had a new client from New Zealand called Skeggs that promoted flash-frozen orange roughie for sale in supermarkets. Together we learned a lot about the process and how it results in a very good product.

"I had always stressed the value of 'fresh only' for the finfish served at The Fort," my father later wrote. Thus, at the Aspen Food and Wine Festival years ago, I was vexed and disbelieving when a salmon salesman from Norway announced that The Fort was serving the fish he sold. I did not know that my chef had been using whole frozen Norwegian salmon. Noting my horror, the sales rep promised to prove to me that what we were serving was as good or better than fresh. We ran some cooking and tasting tests, and the proof was clearly in our mouths. The so-called fresh salmon didn't taste as fresh as the frozen salmon from Norway. The texture of both was identical.

I came to learn that the Sekkingstad family in Bergen, Norway, had been licensed by a Japanese company that had developed a remarkable new freezing technique. At that time, my father noted, they were the only company in Norway to have the proper equipment.

He and my stepmother, Carrie, traveled to Norway to look into the method. The salmon were farmed in fjords that are sometimes 3,000 feet deep and filled with cold, clean water. The fish were harvested when they were three feet long and processed at water's edge, where they went through the freezing process within moments of coming out of the water.

The result is that in Denver, Colorado, in our walk-in cooler, the thawed fish starts out with a very low bacteria count (less than 3 percent), whereas fresh fish arrive with bacteria counts of more than 30 percent. The frozen Norwegian salmon have a longer shelf life, which begins only when the fish are thawed in the cooler, instead of at least two days earlier, as is the case for fresh fish sent from Alaska, Canada, or Chile.

Today at The Fort we pride ourselves on serving the freshest-tasting salmon available. It's easy to determine when fish are fresh if you buy them from a reputable market: First, look at the eyes for clarity. If they are sunken and dull, the fish is old. Next, open the gills with your fingers and make sure they are bright red. Finally, push against the meat of the fish's body with your finger. If the indentation springs back, you have a fresh fish. If the indentation remains in the flesh, look for another fish. And if there is odor other than a faint smell of the sea, move on.

Astrid's Broiled Salmon with Scandinavian Dill Sauce

The Gustermans were close friends of my parents who lived in Georgetown, a small mining hamlet high in the Rockies. My mother had always loved the flavors of fresh dill sauce served with salmon and so asked Astrid for her authentic Swedish recipe; it went right on our menu in the 1960s. This dish is a tribute to Astrid, both for her outstanding cooking and her loyal friendship.

SERVES 4

Ingredients

CUCUMBER DILL SAUCE

1 cup sour cream

1 tablespoon peeled, deseeded, and finely diced cucumber

1 teaspoon chopped fresh dill

5 drops Worcestershire sauce

Dash of salt

SALMON

1 whole salmon or 4 (6–8 ounce) fillets, skin on

4 tbs canola or vegetable oil

4 tablespoons Paprika or 2 tbs cayenne (optional)

Juice of ½ lemon

¼ cup unsalted butter, melted

1 teaspoon dried dill

4 lemon halves

Directions

1. At least eight hours in advance, combine all the sauce ingredients and refrigerate, covered, until serving time.

2. Preheat the oven to broil or heat your grill to high.

3. If you purchase a whole salmon instead of fillets, use a boning knife to cut along the backbone on either side and remove the fillets. Check for small bones near the dorsal fin and any leftover bones you may have missed when filleting. A pair of long-nose tweezers is used by most fish butchers to pull hidden bones. Feel with your fingers and then tweeze them out.

4. Brush the fillets with oil to keep them from sticking to the broiling pan or grill. Dust the flesh side with paprika. Broil or grill 3 to 4 minutes per side, skin side down first. Watch carefully and don't overcook.

5. The skin can be removed from the fillet before serving, but it serves to hold the fish nicely together while it's on the grill. Brush the fillets with lemon juice and butter, and sprinkle them lightly with dried dill. Serve with lemon halves and cucumber dill sauce on the side.

Note: These days many people like their fish nearly raw. It is fashionable to sear the outside and leave the inside barely warm. If that's what you like, cut down the cooking time and put the fillets closer to the heat. The fish needs to be extremely fresh if you are going to cook it this way. Eating raw or undercooked fish can cause food poisoning. I suggest cooking fish until the internal temperature is at 145 degrees, using a food thermometer, to be safe.

Fort Edmonton Canadian Whitefish with Herbed Prairie Butter

When my dad and I visited historic Fort Edmonton near Edmonton, Canada, we learned that the Hudson's Bay Company, which ran The Fort, hired cooks to prepare wonderful meals for traders and soldiers. At Christmastime in 1834, these cooks reportedly served Canadian whitefish sautéed in buffalo bone marrow. Upon hearing this, both Dad and I whipped around and grinned at each other. We could do this! Upon our return to Denver, we began importing fresh whitefish from a Canadian First Nations tribe. It's no longer possible to buy imported Canadian whitefish, but any whitefish, such as arctic char, do very nicely. If you can't find buffalo bones for the marrow, try beef or veal bone marrow. This dish is well worth trying, as it's surprisingly delicious!

SERVES 4

Ingredients

4 (6-ounce) fillets Canadian whitefish or arctic char

½ cup cornmeal

½ cup flour

Salt and pepper, to taste

½ teaspoon cayenne pepper

2 large eggs, beaten

2 tbs olive oil

4 tablespoons Herbed Prairie Butter, divided (recipe follows)

Chopped fresh Italian parsley, for garnish

4 lemon slices, for garnish

Directions

1. Rinse with water and pat dry the fish fillets.

2. Sift the cornmeal, flour, salt, pepper, and cayenne together. Brush the fillets with the beaten eggs, then dredge them in the cornmeal/flour mixture.

3. Heat olive oil and 2 tablespoons of herbed butter in a sauté pan over medium-high heat and place the fillets. Cover and cook for 3 to 4 minutes. Turn the fillets, cover again, and cook for another 3 to 4 minutes.

4. Place fillets on a serving plate and garnish with the remaining herbed butter, fresh parsley, and lemon slices. This fish is delicious served with wild rice or quinoa.

Herbed Prairie Butter

Ingredients

1 buffalo femur bone, split, or 2 bones beef or veal marrow bones, split

¼ pound Herb Butter (page 140)

Directions

1. Preheat the oven to 500°F. Arrange the bones in a shallow roasting pan and roast for 15 to 20 minutes. Allow the bones to cool slightly, then scoop out the marrow and chop it roughly.

2. Put the butter and marrow in an electric mixer bowl, and whip on medium speed until the marrow is incorporated into the butter.

3. Remove the butter from the mixer and place it on cooking parchment to roll into cylinders. Refrigerate or freeze the cylinders for later use.

Great Lakes Walleye with Lemon Cream Sauce

In 2019, The Fort's chefs discovered the Great Lakes walleye, a distant cousin to pike and a delicious, meaty whitefish that the French-Canadian voyagers would cook in the early 1800s. Our guests have been delighted by the flavor of walleye, and this recipe has become a favorite.

Ingredients

1 cup heavy cream

8 tablespoons (1 stick) unsalted butter

2 tablespoons lemon juice

1 tablespoon minced garlic

¼ cup diced leeks

1 teaspoon dried basil

Salt and freshly ground pepper, to taste

2 walleye 6-8 ounce fillets

1 tablespoon paprika

4 lemon slices

1 tablespoon chopped parsley

Directions

1. Preheat the oven to 425°F.

2. In a saucepan over medium heat, combine the heavy cream, butter, lemon juice, garlic, leeks, basil, and salt and pepper. Bring to a boil and allow the sauce to reduce for 5 minutes. Lower the heat to warm. Set aside.

3. Place the walleye on an oil sprayed sheet pan. Dust the walleye with paprika and place the lemon slices on top of the fish. Cover the fish with half of the lemon cream sauce and bake in the center of the oven for 10 to 12 minutes, at which point the sauce will have browned slightly.

4. Plate the fish and top with the remaining sauce. Garnish with the parsley.

Crispy Cod with Homemade Tartar Sauce

This is another new creation by The Fort's chefs and an old-fashioned East Coast favorite. Served at the restaurant on Mother's Day in 2019, this recipe had rave reviews!

SERVES 4

Ingredients

FISH AND BREADING

½ cup egg yolks, or 8 egg yolks

2 cups panko breadcrumbs

1 tsp dried sage

½ tsp granulated garlic

½ tsp dried oregano

1 tsp salt

1 tsp freshly ground pepper

Spray of canola oil (30 seconds)

4 cod 6 ounce fillets

TARTAR SAUCE

1 cup mayonnaise

¼ cup pickle relish

1 tablespoon dill

¼ cup lemon juice

1 teaspoon salt

1 tsp freshly ground pepper

Directions

1. Preheat the oven to 425°F. Beat egg yolks in a medium bowl until well blended.

2. Mix breadcrumbs, sage, garlic, oregano, and salt and pepper in a blender to a fine consistency. Place breadcrumb mixture on 9" x 12" sheet of parchment paper on a flat surface. Place bowl with egg yolk mixture next to the parchment paper. Spray a 8" x 8" baking dish with canola oil.

3. Dip the cod fillets in the egg yolks, then dip it into the breading mixture, coating on all sides. Place in baking dish.

4. Bake the breaded fish for 10 to 12 minutes.

5. Mix all tartar sauce ingredients until incorporated. Adjust with more lemon juice as necessary.

6. Serve the fish with tartar sauce on the side.

THE SCOOP ON SHRIMP

We serve shrimp at The Fort, not because they are caught anywhere nearby but because they are so loved by many of our customers and lend themselves to so many remarkable preparations. They are sized according the how many headless, raw shrimp there are in a pound. For instance, U/10 means there are 10 or fewer shrimp in the pound weight. We use in most dishes, the U-10, or also known as Extra Colossal Shrimp, at The Fort. When it comes to commercial names, for extra jumbo shrimp expect 16 to 20 of the crustaceans in a pound; extra-large shrimp, 26/30; and medium shrimp, 25 to 31.

Gulf Shrimp en Globo

My dad observed that when shrimp are broiled over a hot grill, they lose so much moisture that they shrink into unappetizing specimens, and so he came up with a dish he dubbed Gulf Shrimp en Globo. Five or six shrimp, dabbed with a little herb butter, are encased in an aluminum foil packet that balloons during cooking and renders the shrimp moist and tender. Besides its glorious flavor, I love that this dish can be prepared in advance. After cleaning the shrimp, making the herb butter, and then sealing the shrimp in foil, the packets can be refrigerated until it is time to cook them.

SERVES 4

Ingredients

6 fresh basil leaves

8 sprigs Italian parsley

2 cloves garlic, crushed

Juice of ½ lemon

4–6 tablespoons unsalted butter

16 squares aluminum foil, each approximately 10 inches square

2 pounds Gulf white shrimp as large as you can find, peeled and deveined

4 cups cooked white rice (optional)

Directions

1. Using a mortar and pestle or food processor, blend the basil, parsley, garlic, lemon juice, and butter. Set aside.

2. For each serving, lay 2 squares of aluminum foil on top of each other and fold their edges so that they are securely attached. Double layering prevents spillage and breaking. Divide the shrimp and herb butter among the 4 foil packets. Cover each packet with 2 additional sheets of foil, fold over the edges, and seal well. Store in the refrigerator for a few hours until ready to use or freeze for later use.

3. When ready to cook, preheat the grill. Turn the heat to medium and place the foil packets over the fire for about 5 minutes, until they puff up, then remove from the fire. If the shrimp are frozen, they will have to cook for another 3 minutes until done.

4. Snip the foil with scissors to easily remove the shrimp from the packets. They're delicious over a bed of rice, if desired. Or serve in the closed packets and allow your guests to open them at the table.

Chipotle-Skewered Shrimp

The smokiness of the chipotle blends beautifully with grilled shrimp so that these become a simply irresistible appetizer or main course. The shrimp are a popular request for private parties at The Fort, where we pass them as appetizers.

SERVES 4

Ingredients

4 bamboo or metal skewers

½ cup olive oil

1 clove garlic, peeled and minced

Juice of 1 lemon (about 3 tablespoons)

3 dashes of chipotle sauce or ½ teaspoon mashed chipotle pepper in adovada sauce

1 teaspoon honey or sugar (optional)

20 jumbo shrimp with tail on, peeled and deveined

1 recipe Rice Pilaf (page 120)

Fresh cilantro or Italian parsley sprigs, for garnish

Directions

1. If you are using bamboo skewers, let them soak in water while you prepare the sauce so they won't burn on the grill.

2. About 1 hour before cooking, whisk together the olive oil, garlic, lemon juice, and chipotle sauce in a medium sized bowl. Adding a teaspoon of honey or sugar to the sauce will give the shrimp a slight caramelized glaze, if you wish.

3. Add the shrimp to the sauce, cover and allow to marinate in the refrigerator for 1 hour.

4. Preheat a charcoal grill to medium. Thread the head and tail of each shrimp onto a bamboo skewer, 5 per skewer, and grill for 2 minutes, brushing with the sauce while they cook. Serve on a bed of pilaf. A sprig or two of cilantro or parsley makes a nice garnish.

On-the-Beach Steamed Giant Gulf Shrimp

Although these steamed shrimp were on the menu during the early days of The Fort, I fondly remember eating them on the beach in Corpus Christi, Texas. I was 18, and my dad, my brother, and I built a fire on the beach. We filled a pot with beer, added a few bay leaves and some salt and pepper, and then dumped the jumbo shrimp, still in their shells, into the pot. A few minutes later, we pulled the shrimp out, shelled them, and dipped the slightly smoky, beer-flavored shrimp in melted butter spiked with lemon juice. Naturally, we had another six-pack of cold beer to drink with our shrimp. So delish!

SERVES 4–6

Ingredients

2 pounds colossal (4-inch) shrimp in their shells

6-pack stout beer

4 bay leaves

¼ cup Old Bay Seasoning for seafood

1 tablespoon black pepper, or to taste

Sea salt, to taste

8 tablespoons (1 stick) unsalted butter, melted

Juice of 1 lemon (about 3 tablespoons)

Directions

1. If the shrimp are frozen, place the block of shrimp in cool water in a sink for 1 hour or until defrosted. Using a small, sharp knife, make a ½-inch-deep cut down the back of each shrimp. Rinse the shrimp under cold water and remove the vein but leave the shell on.

2. In a stockpot, combine the beer, bay leaves, dry seasoning, pepper, and salt. Bring the beer to a boil over high heat. Add the shrimp and reduce the heat to low. Steam the shrimp until the shells turn pink and the flesh turns opaque, no more than 3 to 4 minutes for Colossal shrimp. Do not overcook! Remove them from the beer with a slotted spoon.

3. Combine the lemon juice and butter. Serve the shrimp with lemon butter for dipping.

TORTILLAS

In Spain, a tortilla is a potato omelet. In Mexico, tortillas are pliable flatbreads, just as most Americans think of them. Because I live in the Southwest and not Spain, I am interested in only the latter. These flatbreads are amazingly versatile, and at The Fort we rely on them for myriad dishes.

There are two kinds of tortillas, defined by their ingredients. Wheat tortillas, most popular in northern Mexico and southern New Mexico and Arizona where wheat is grown, usually measure between 6 and 12 inches in diameter and may be as thick as half an inch when leavened with yeast or baking powder. They are mild tasting and pale in color.

Corn tortillas generally are smaller than wheat, rarely measuring larger than six inches across and often less. They are made from cornmeal ground from corn kernels first cooked in slaked lime (calcium hydroxide), which removes the tough outer skin of the corn. Their flavor is immediately recognizable as coming from corn and blends deliciously with any number of southwestern ingredients.

Both kinds of tortillas are baked on a flat griddle or grill. The most authentic device for cooking them is a comal, a flat pan used throughout Mexico that resembles a skillet or griddle and is used for tortillas as well as to toast spices. In much of South America, the same pan is called a budare. If you don't have a comal, you can bake tortillas in skillets, on iron griddles, or even on a sheet of steel set over a source of heat.

If you like to make yeast bread, you can make flour tortillas. Make the dough, form some into a ball about the size of a small apple, and then, using a rolling pin, roll the dough into a flat, thin round about eight inches in diameter. Heat a skillet or comal over medium heat, sprinkle the hot surface with about half a teaspoon of salt to prevent sticking, and then panfry the tortilla until lightly browned and still flexible. Turn and fry the other side.

Lobster and Shrimp Enchilada Suiza

During the 1960s, my father's famous chicken enchilada Suiza was on the menu, and I loved it. When I was about 10 years old, I remember asking the chef to make it for me and pack it up so that I could take it to the top of the 90-foot red rock next to the restaurant and eat it while watching a spectacular Rocky Mountain sunset. Years later, my son Oren made it and called it Orenchilada, and the *Denver Post* wrote a feature story about it. I have altered the recipe so that now it's made with lobster and shrimp—and richer and more seductive than ever.

I make this with rock lobster, also called langouste, not to be confused with Maine lobsters, which have big claws. The langouste grows in both warm and cold water but the best is found in the chilly waters off the coasts of Australia and New Zealand.

SERVES 6

Ingredients

4 tablespoons unsalted butter

2 tablespoons all-purpose flour

2 cups (1 pint) light cream or half-and-half

1 clove garlic, crushed

1½ teaspoons dried Mexican oregano

½ teaspoon salt

1 cup sour cream

12 corn tortillas

½ pound uncooked shrimp, peeled, cleaned, and deveined

½ pound raw lobster meat

1 yellow onion, finely chopped

1½ cups chopped mild green chiles, fresh or canned

½ cup chopped walnuts, lightly toasted

½ cup sliced ripe black olives

2 cups grated Monterey Jack cheese

2 cups grated sharp cheddar cheese

Avocado wedges, strips of red pimento, black and green olives, or toasted walnuts or pine nuts for garnish (optional)

Directions

1. Preheat the oven to 350°F.

2. In a large saucepan, melt butter over medium heat. Add the flour and cook, stirring for 1 minute. Gradually whisk in the cream, and add the garlic, oregano, and salt. Cook, stirring, for about 1 minute, until the sauce begins to thicken. Remove from heat and whisk in the sour cream.

3. Line a 9- to 10-inch, shallow buttered casserole with half of the corn tortillas. Overlap them to cover the bottom and sides completely. Scatter half of the shrimp and half of the lobster over the tortillas, then half of the onion, chiles, walnuts, and olives. Pour over 1 cup of the warm sauce. Combine the cheeses and sprinkle half over the casserole.

4. Repeat the process with the remaining ingredients, beginning with the corn tortillas and finishing with the cheese.

5. Bake for about 1½ hours, until well heated. When the cheese bubbles and becomes golden brown, the enchilada is ready to eat. If your casserole is deeper than it is wide, the enchilada may take longer to cook all the way through. In this case, when the cheese has browned, cover the dish with aluminum foil and continue to bake. Garnish as you like with avocado, pimento, olives, or toasted nuts.

Three-Legged Lobster with Lemon Butter

As my dad once said, "One of the joys of lobster, scallops, and crab is that when they're grilled, the slightly burned taste much improves their overall flavor." This recipe calls for browning and then arranging the lobster for a presentation your guests will not soon forget. It works best for lobster tails that weigh at least eight ounces.

SERVES 4

Ingredients

4 (8-ounce or larger) lobster tails

8 tablespoons unsalted butter, melted, divided

Juice of ½ lemon

Sprinkle of paprika

2 lemons or sweet limes, halved

Directions

1. Preheat the grill to medium. Mix the melted butter and lemon juice and set aside.

2. Place the lobster tail on the counter so that it rests on the shell. Using kitchen scissors, cut along the lower edge of the shell to remove the bottom cover skin. Reach between the meat and the shell to gently loosen the entire tail, leaving the extreme back end attached. With a sharp knife, slit the meat lengthwise up the middle, making two "legs" of the meat. Brush these with 4 ounces of lemon butter and a little sprinkle of paprika.

OYSTERS IN SANTA FE

Susan Shelby Magoffin was one of the first Anglo women to come across the Santa Fe Trail in 1846, traveling with her trader husband, Samuel Magoffin. She kept a diary that the Yale University Press still prints today in which she describes eating oysters on the half shell and drinking the finest French champagne at a party in Santa Fe. Where did they get fresh oysters in land-locked Santa Fe? They pulled them from the Chesapeake Bay; layered the live oysters in large oak casks, their "mouths" facing upward; and then covered them with shaved ice and cornmeal. As the wagon train traveled from one town to the next, the drivers replenished the ice and cornmeal to keep the oysters alive and well fed. Week by week, month by month, town by town, eventually the wagon train arrived in Santa Fe with plump, living oysters ready to be shucked and eaten with chilled Champagne.

3. Lay the meat on the grill and cook on low to medium heat for approximately 4 minutes. When the tails have browned a bit, turn over and brown the other side, for approximately 2-3 minutes.

4. When the meat is opaque and cooked through, remove the tails to a serving plate. Stand them up to a tripod of shell and both "legs" of meat. Place a small cup of the remaining 4 ounces of lemon butter in front of each lobster tail, beside half a lemon or sweet lime wrapped in a square of cheesecloth twisted at the top and tied with a piece of string.

Vegetarian Main Courses

Thomas Jefferson's Green Chile Mac & Cheese Savory "Pudding"

Researching historical recipes, I found in the *American Heritage* cookbook, that President Thomas Jefferson had discovered a delicious savory "pudding" in France and decided to bring it to America and serve this "pudding" in the White House in 1803. It was Macaroni and Cheese "pudding." The French version was made with a white bechamel sauce and gruyere cheese. The American version, President Jefferson served, was made with cheddar, as I expect it was because the former British colonists made cheddar cheese, and it was readily available. At The Fort, we decided to incorporate the French version using gruyere cheese, but also add New Mexican green chiles, and other Mexican cheeses to our sauce. There are ledger records that macaroni pasta was sold at the original Bent's Old Fort in southern Colorado in 1833- only 30 years after President Jefferson started the trend. We get rave reviews for TJ's Macaroni & Cheese "Pudding" nightly from guests at The Fort.

SERVES 4-6

Ingredients

4 cups macaroni noodles

4 tablespoons (½ stick) unsalted butter

½ cup all-purpose flour

1 cup buttermilk

2 cups heavy cream

3 cups shredded gruyère cheese

1 cup chopped green chiles

Salt and freshly ground pepper, to taste

2 cups mixed shredded cheese blend (Monterey Jack, Oaxaca, manchego, asadero)

Directions

1. In a large pot of lightly salted boiling water, cook noodles for approximately 7 minutes or until desired doneness. Drain noodles, but do not rinse.

2. Preheat the oven to 425°F. In a saucepan, melt butter over medium heat. Whisk flour into butter, making a roux. Cook roux for 5 minutes, stirring constantly. Meanwhile, in a separate saucepan, over medium heat, bring buttermilk and cream to a simmer. Whisk hot cream mixture into roux and simmer, stirring constantly, until the sauce thickens.

3. Reduce the heat to low and add gruyère, stirring until fully incorporated. Add noodles and green chiles to sauce. Season to taste with salt and pepper.

4. Place noodle and sauce mixture in a cast-iron baking dish. Top with shredded cheese. Bake for 8 to 10 minutes, until desired brownness has been achieved.

Roasted Bell Peppers with Wild Mushroom Risotto

Both colorful and delicious, this vegetarian entrée celebrates the garden and forest bounty! It was The Fort's seasonal vegetarian entrée in 2020.

Ingredients

2 cups chopped shitake mushrooms

2 tablespoons olive oil

2 cups arborio rice

3 cups vegetable stock

1 cup dry white wine

½ tablespoon fresh thyme

Salt and freshly ground pepper, to taste

½ cup corn kernels, fresh or frozen

½ cup diced onions

½ cup cooked Anasazi beans (canned)

½ cup toasted pepitas

4 red bell peppers, halved length wise, and insides cleaned

2 cups shredded pepper jack cheese

Directions

1. In a large sauté pan, add the olive oil and heat the pan to medium heat. Add the mushrooms, onions, thyme, and sauté, stirring occasionally, to let the onions and mushrooms caramelize. Add rice, and 1 cup of vegetable stock and ½ cup of wine, until absorbed, stirring constantly. Add another cup of stock and the remaining wine, until absorbed, stirring until absorbed. Add the final cup of stock and continue to stir until completely absorbed. Add salt and freshly ground pepper to taste. Add the corn, onions, Anasazi beans, and pepitas to the risotto mixture and cook until heated through.

2. Preheat the oven to 425 degrees.

3. Spray a baking pan with canola oil, and lightly spray the uncooked halved bell peppers (optional- may keep the green stem, halved, or remove. The peppers are the edible "dish") with oil. Place peppers in the pan and roast in the hot oven for 15 minutes. Remove from oven and let cool for 5-8 minutes.

4. Fill the bell peppers with the risotto mixture. Top with the pepper jack cheese and bake for 8 to 10 minutes more to melt and brown the cheese. Serve two halves per person. This dish pairs well with the Quinoa Salad with Fresh Garden Mint (page 90).

Three Sacred Sisters Tamale Pie

Because I was a strict vegetarian in the 1970s and 80s—almost vegan—I know how tough it is to find a good vegetarian entrée in a restaurant celebrated for its meat. This tamale pie gives the most succulent buffalo tenderloin a run for its money! It's an aromatic, complete protein dish and when it's carried to the table, meat lovers crane their necks to get a better view. The pie includes the corn, beans, and squash that are representative of the Indian diet and that for generations have been referred to as the three sacred sisters.

SERVES 4-6

Ingredients

VEGETABLES

2 tablespoons olive or canola oil

1 cup chopped yellow onion (1 small)

2 teaspoons minced garlic (2 cloves)

2 teaspoons mild to medium ground New Mexican red chile

1½ teaspoons ground cumin

1 teaspoon dried Mexican oregano

2 cups corn kernels, fresh or frozen

1 cup chopped mild green chiles, fresh or canned

1½ cups vegetable broth

½ cup fire-roasted tomato purée

2 cups cooked Anasazi beans or pinto beans (15-ounce can, rinsed and drained)

2 cups finely diced zucchini (2–3 small zucchini)

Salt and freshly ground pepper, to taste

MASA CRUST

1½ cups masa harina de maize (corn tortilla mix)

1½ teaspoons baking powder

½ teaspoon salt

¼ cup vegetable shortening

1–1¼ cups warm vegetable broth or water

1½ cups shredded Monterey Jack and Colby cheese mix

Directions

1. To make the vegetables: Place oil in a large sauté pan or skillet over medium heat. Add the onion and garlic and cook, stirring, over medium-low heat, for 3 to 5 minutes, until onion is softened and translucent. Stir in the ground chile, cumin, and oregano. Add the corn and green chiles and stir in vegetable broth and tomato purée. Add the beans and zucchini, and simmer over medium heat for about 5 minutes, until zucchini is slightly tender (al dente). Taste and season with salt and pepper.

2. To make the crust : In a mixing bowl, combine masa harina, baking powder, and salt. In a food processor with a steel knife blade, beat shortening until fluffy. Add masa mixture and pulse on and off a few times. Add the warm broth and pulse on and off until dough comes together.

3. Divide the vegetable mixture among 4 to 6 oven-safe serving dishes and top with masa dough. Bake 10 to 15 minutes, until lightly browned. Top with shredded cheese and bake another 3 to 5 minutes, until cheese is golden.

Quick Vegetarian Posole

I was so taken by a vegetarian posole made during a cooking demonstration at The Fort, I had to come up with my own version. The original was delicious and was cooked in a micaceous clay pot by Charlie and Debbie Carrillo from Santa Fe. He is an artist from that New Mexico city and a santero, or carver of saints. To enhance this soup a little, serve it with sour cream or shredded Monterey Jack cheese.

SERVES 6

Ingredients

1½ cups chopped red onion (1 medium)

1 cup chopped red bell pepper (1 large)

2–3 teaspoons minced fresh garlic (2–3 cloves)

1–2 tablespoons canola or olive oil

1 tablespoon New Mexican ground red chile (Dixon preferred)

4 cups vegetable broth

1 (29-ounce) can Mexican-style hominy, drained and rinsed

1 (14 ½-ounce) can fire-roasted diced tomatoes with medium green chiles

Salt and freshly ground pepper, to taste

Fresh cilantro sprigs, for garnish (optional)

Directions

1. In a large sauté pan or skillet, over medium-high heat, sauté onion, red pepper, and garlic in oil until onion is translucent. Reduce heat to medium-low, add the ground chile, and cook, stirring, for 2 minutes. Stir in the vegetable broth. Add hominy (posole) and tomatoes and bring to a boil. Reduce heat to low and simmer for 20 minutes.

2. Season the soup with salt and pepper to taste. Ladle the hot posole into bowls and garnish with cilantro, if desired.

WHAT'S A TAMALE?

Tamales are nearly always individual servings made from a base of cornmeal (masa harina) and wrapped in leaves that are discarded before eating. The leaves most often are corn husks but can be banana leaves or something similar. Tamales usually are steamed, although they also may be baked. The cornmeal base is mixed with any number of ingredients, from squash, beans, chiles, and mushrooms to shredded meat or poultry. The mixture generally is highly seasoned, although not necessarily spicy. Mexican tamales tend to be a little lighter in texture than Tex-Mex tamales, and preferences for one or the other are purely personal. These are rarely small bites but substantial servings that are lovingly handcrafted and meant to be enjoyed with gusto.

Vegetarian Nacatamales

When I was at the International Fancy Food Show about 20 years ago, I discovered a company from Oaxaca, Mexico, that exported vegetarian tamales wrapped in banana leaves. We imported them for The Fort until 2001, when the company stopped exporting them, but because our customers were wild about them, we developed our own recipe. They were our top-selling vegetarian entrée and were popular served alongside buffalo or quail.

MAKES 12 TAMALES; SERVES 4–6

Ingredients

MASA

3 cups masa harina de maize (corn tortilla mix)

1½ tablespoons baking powder

1 teaspoon salt

½ cup vegetable shortening

2½–3 cups warm vegetable broth or water

ANCHO CHILE SAUCE

3 dried ancho chiles

1 clove garlic, peeled

½ teaspoon dried Mexican oregano

½ teaspoon salt, plus more to taste

2 whole cloves

2 whole peppercorns

1 tablespoon olive oil

CALABACITA (MEXICAN SQUASH) FILLING

3 tablespoons olive oil

1½ cups chopped carrots

¾ cup chopped red onion

3 large cloves garlic, peeled and minced

3–4 small calabacitas (or yellow squash and/or zucchini), chopped (about 2 cups)

3 plum tomatoes, cored and chopped

1 small bunch spinach (about 20 leaves), rinsed and chopped

Salt, to taste

1 pound fresh or frozen banana leaves

12 ounces Monterey Jack cheese, cut into 12 (4 x ½-inch) strips

Equipment needed: A large steamer or a stockpot with a steamer rack, kitchen twine

1. Prepare the masa: Combine the masa harina, baking powder, and salt in a mixing bowl. With an electric mixer, beat shortening in a separate bowl until fluffy. Add 1 cup of the masa harina mixture and 1 cup of warm broth to the shortening and beat until well combined. Continue adding dry ingredients and broth until all are mixed and the dough has a smooth consistency.

2. Prepare the sauce (steps 2–6): Rinse the chiles under warm water and use a paring knife to slit them down one side. Open the chiles and remove the seeds and veins. Add seeds to the mix if you want more heat!

3. Place a griddle or large skillet over medium heat. Flatten out the dried chiles and place them on the griddle. Press down on the open chiles and leave for a few seconds. Turn the chiles over and repeat. Do not toast or burn the chiles, just heat them until the rinsing water evaporates.

4. Place the chiles in a small saucepan and add enough water to cover. Bring to a boil. Remove from heat and let sit for 10 minutes, until the chiles have softened and plumped up.

5. Reserving the soaking water, remove the chiles from the pan and place in a blender. Add the garlic, oregano, ½ teaspoon salt, cloves, peppercorns, and 1½ cups of the soaking liquid. Blend until the sauce is completely smooth. Taste the sauce and adjust the seasoning. If you want more heat, add a few of the seeds or veins and blend some more. Taste, and add additional salt if needed.

6. Press the sauce through a sieve into a skillet. Add 1 tablespoon of olive oil to the sauce. Bring to a simmer and reduce heat to maintain the simmer. Cook for 10 minutes, stirring occasionally. Skim off the foam that rises to the top. Remove sauce from heat and reserve.

7. Prepare the calabacita filling: Coat the bottom of a sauté pan with olive oil and place over medium heat. Add the carrots, onion, and garlic to the hot skillet. Sauté for 2 to 3 minutes, until the onion begins to soften, and then add squash and tomatoes and cook 1 minute. Add the spinach and cook, stirring, until just wilted. Remove from heat. Stir ½ cup of ancho chile sauce into the sautéed vegetables, and season to taste with salt.

8. Prepare the banana leaves: If you are using frozen banana leaves (available at many Asian and Mexican markets), rinse them under warm water to defrost. Cut away the thick edges of the leaves. If you are using fresh banana leaves, cut away the thick edges and the central stem . Rinse the fresh leaves under warm water. Banana leaves may be brittle and tear when you try to fold them. One way I've heard of to soften them is to soak them in warm, salted water for about an hour. Another way, which I have found effective, is to hold them over a gas burner or place them on a hot griddle for a few seconds until they turn color (brighter green) and soften. If you heat them too long, they will toast and become brittle again. Cut the banana leaves into 8x10-inch rectangles and pat them dry with paper towels.

9. Assemble the tamales (steps 9–12): Banana leaves have two sides. One side, the top of the leaf, is deep green and has somewhat thick ridges. The other side, the bottom of the leaf, is lighter green and is smoother. You will want to place the masa on the lighter green, smoother side of the leaf.

10. Lay out a rectangle of banana leaf, light side up. Place ¼ to ⅓ cup of masa on the center of the banana leaf. Press down on the masa with the palm of your hand to spread it out a bit.

11. Spread 1 teaspoon of ancho chili sauce over the masa. Place a strip of Monterey Jack cheese on top. Place about ¼ cup of the calabacita mixture on top of the cheese.

12. Bring together the two long sides of the banana leaf and fold over, tucking one edge over the other. Fold the two remaining sides under the tamale. Secure with kitchen string or a strip of banana leaf. Or, you can skip the tying step altogether and just fold it well. Repeat steps 10–12 for the remaining 11 tamales.

13. Steam the tamales: Add enough water to the steamer to come almost up to the level of the rack. Place extra banana leaves in the bottom of the steamer basket.

14. Carefully arrange the tamales in layers on the bottom of the pan. When you have added all of the tamales, add another layer of banana leaves. Cover the pot.

15. Bring water to a boil, then reduce heat to a simmer. Steam the tamales for approximately 1 hour.

Holly's Sweet Cupboard and Icehouse

Mexican Chocolate Ice Cream Mud Pie

To make the best mud pie, you need the BEST ice cream! Magill's Creamery in Colorado is *the* best, and they make this special Mexican chocolate ice cream for The Fort. Each summer, we hold a culinary competition for our cooks and this recipe was awarded first place and put on the menu in 2013. It has become one of our most popular desserts!

SERVES 8

Ingredients

8 tablespoons unsalted butter, melted

1¾ cup Oreo cookie crumbs

1 cup tart dried cherries

2 cups cherry liqueur

¼ cup coffee liqueur

½ gallon Mexican chocolate ice cream

⅓ gallon coffee ice cream

2 cups toffee pieces

Directions

1. Preheat oven to 350°F.

2. Mix melted butter and Oreo crumbs in a bowl until fully incorporated. In a 9" springform pan, spread mixture evenly and press into the bottom. Bake for 5 to 8 minutes to set the crust. Set aside to cool.

3. Soak cherries in hot water for 30 minutes, then drain the water. Marinate cherries in cherry liqueur for another 30 minutes, then drain the liqueur.

4. Drizzle the cooled crust with coffee liqueur and add the drained cherries evenly over the bottom.

5. Take ice cream out of the freezer and let soften at room temperature for 15 minutes. Mix the softened Mexican chocolate ice cream and coffee ice cream in a medium bowl in a stand mixer using the bread paddle. Mix on medium speed until both ice creams are well blended- about 5 minutes. Immediately spread the ice cream mixture over the cherries and top with toffee chunks. Wrap pie with plastic film and freeze for up to 3 hours. Remove from freezer 20 minutes before serving, and let stand, at room temperature, to allow for the "Pie" to soften before cutting.

Cider-Cooked Trappers' Fruit

It comes as no surprise that both the early trappers and soldiers, as well as the Native Americans, relied heavily on dried fruits to get them through the winter. The fruits were accompanied by other dried foods—such as buffalo jerky, buffalo fat, and gathered nuts—as survival foods. Indians often subsisted on a mixture of fat, dried meat, nuts, and fruits called pemmican, and while it may not appeal to our modern palates, it was a nutritious substitute for a substantial meal; traders, trappers, and the army often turned to pemmican, too. We don't serve pemmican at The Fort; instead we make this dried fruit compote to accompany meat or, more often, to spoon over ice cream. As the dried apples, spices, hazelnuts, and rum cook, the compote just turns more syrupy, mellow, dark, and delicious.

SERVES 8

Ingredients

½ cup coarsely chopped hazelnuts, toasted

4 quarts apple cider

2 pounds dried apples

2 cups applesauce

3 tablespoons brown sugar or honey

½ cup fresh lemon juice

1 tablespoon coriander seeds

½ teaspoon ground cinnamon

½ teaspoon ground cloves

½ teaspoon grated nutmeg

½ cup golden raisins

1 tablespoon vanilla extract

1 cup dark rum (Myers's preferred)

Directions

Combine all ingredients except the rum in a large pot and bring to a boil over high heat. Lower the heat, cover, and simmer for at least 1 hour to reduce the liquid. Trappers' Fruit will be ready to eat whenever you're ready to eat it. (At The Fort we like to cook it, covered, for several hours, stirring frequently to prevent burning.) Just before serving, add the rum.

Vera's Caramel–Canola Seed Brownies

Our guests love these brownies and without doubt you will, too—if you like fudgy, chocolaty treats! My dad wrote about these brownies, recalling a telephone call he got out of the blue in 1998 from a woman named Vera Dahlquist. Would he consider hiring a baker who was 80 years old? she asked. "You bet I would!" Dad said. "She probably knows more about baking than the rest of us put together." Vera, who had emigrated from Finland as a child, was a gifted baker and we all enjoyed her banana cream pies and fragrant dinner rolls, but our very favorite were these brownies. They have a chewiness that makes them both a brownie and a candy. To achieve this glorious texture, hand-mix the batter rather than relying on an electric mixer so that you don't beat too much air into it.

MAKES 15 LARGE BROWNIES

Ingredients

2½ cups all-purpose flour

3 cups brown sugar

3 teaspoons baking powder

¼ teaspoon salt

4 large eggs

20 tablespoons (2 ½ sticks) unsalted butter or margarine, melted

1 teaspoon vanilla extract

1 cup chopped walnuts or pecans

¼ cup toasted canola seeds

Directions

1. Preheat the oven to 350°F. Grease and line a 9x13-inch baking pan with parchment paper.

2. In a large bowl, blend the flour, brown sugar, baking powder, and salt. In a small bowl, beat the eggs slightly. Stir in the butter and vanilla extract. Add the egg mixture to the dry ingredients and blend well. Stir in the nuts and seeds.

3. Spread the batter in the prepared pan. Bake for 25 to 30 minutes or until the center can be touched without leaving an indentation. Do not overbake!

Biscochitos

These delicate, anise-flavored cookies are indulgently rich, yet still light. Plus, they are easy to make. The cookie was brought to the Southwest by the Spanish in the early 1600s and, like most traditional recipes, there are nearly as many versions as families who claim them as their own. It's so popular that New Mexico declared the biscochito its official state cookie in 1989. I have been eating the cookies all my life, partly because they are so common in this part of the world and also because my father had a special fondness for them. In 1948 he attended a prayer ceremony and midnight mass at a pueblo near Santa Fe called San Felipe, where he tried his first biscochito.

MAKES 6-8 DOZEN COOKIES

Ingredients

6 large eggs

1 pound lard or vegetable shortening

4 to 4 ½ cups sifted all-purpose flour

2 cups sugar

2 tablespoons aniseed

½ half cup rum or bourbon

2 tbs ground cinnamon

Directions

1. Preheat the oven to 350°F.

2. Beat eggs. In another large bowl, mix shortening with sugar. Cream sugar with the shortening until well blended, about 3 minutes. Slowly add 4 cups of flour, into the shortening mixture. Add in eggs, aniseed and the extra flour if needed, to make a firm dough.

3. Roll out the dough to no more than ½" thickness. The cookies should be very thin. Cut the dough into your favorite cookie shapes. Rub the tops of the cookies with rum or bourbon, then sprinkle with cinnamon. Bake for 3 to 5 minutes or until barely brown. These cookies are perfect with hot cider, steaming coffee, or Mexican hot chocolate.

CHRISTMAS FAROLITOS

Santa Fe, New Mexico, celebrates Christmas brilliantly, and one of my favorite customs is that the narrow, ancient streets are illuminated with thousands of farolitos, little paper bag lanterns filled with sand and a lit candle. The cool winter nights glow with their soft light and the crisp air is perfumed with the smoke from cedar and pine nut fires. Walking through the old city is nothing short of magical.

At The Fort, we celebrate the winter holidays starting in November, when we light farolitos in our courtyard. On Christmas Eve, the Tesoro Cultural Center celebrates in much the same way. At both events, we serve biscochito cookies and hot, mulled apple cider.

Gunny's Brandied Pumpkin Pie

My mother thought this was the best pumpkin pie she had ever eaten—and I have to say I agree. Since we first made it in the 1960s, it's been one of my favorites and I can't let a Thanksgiving go by without it, nor can I make a pumpkin pie without brandy. It's an old Pennsylvania Dutch recipe from my father's grandmother, Gunny, who lived in Pennsylvania.

MAKES TWO 9-INCH PIES

Ingredients

1 cup pumpkin

1 (8-ounce) can evaporated milk or 1 cup heavy cream

1 cup sugar

3 large eggs, slightly beaten

4 tablespoons brandy

1 teaspoon ground cinnamon

1 teaspoon grated nutmeg

¾ teaspoon ground ginger

¾ teaspoon salt

¼ teaspoon ground mace

2 (9-inch) frozen pie crusts

Directions

1. Preheat cookie sheet while preheating oven to 375°F.

2. Mix all filling ingredients together and pour half into each crust.

3. Turn the oven temperature down to 350°F and bake the pies on the cookie sheet for about 45 minutes or until the pies don't shake in the center.

Chile-Chocolate Bourbon Cake

While this cake started as the house cake for birthday and anniversary celebrations, customer demand convinced us to put it on the menu as an everyday offering. We still serve a complimentary slice to anyone marking a special occasion at The Fort—and set a ceremonial headdress on their head, too, as the staff shouts, "Hip, hip, huzzah!" We don't do anything halfway at our restaurant!

We make the cake with a little red chile to honor the ancient Aztec tradition of spiking their drinking chocolate with a little heat. This makes sense when you remember that it wasn't until the Europeans took chocolate back to the Old World that anyone thought to sweeten it. Before then, it was made into a bitter, but much appreciated, ceremonial brew. You'll feel a slight burn at the back of the throat when you eat this, but that will quickly turn into a warm glow. The bourbon-flavored frosting adds its own kick.

SERVES 12

Ingredients

CAKE

1–2 tablespoons New Mexican medium ground red chile powder (Dixon preferred), to taste

2 cups water, divided

1 tablespoon pure vanilla extract

1 cup plus 2 tablespoons all-purpose flour

1 cup plus 2 tablespoons cake flour (not self-rising)

2 cups sugar

1 teaspoon baking soda

½ teaspoon salt

½ cup unsweetened, nonalkalized cocoa powder, such as Hershey, Nestlé, or Ghirardelli (do not use Dutch process)

4 tablespoons unsalted butter, softened

½ cup buttermilk

2 large eggs, at room temperature

FROSTING

12 tablespoons unsalted butter

¾ cup unsweetened, nonalkalized cocoa powder

¼ cup plus 2 tablespoons buttermilk

4–5 cups confectioners' sugar, to taste

2–3 tablespoons bourbon, to taste

1 tablespoon pure vanilla extract

1½ cups chopped walnuts, lightly toasted (optional)

Directions

1. For the cake (steps 1–5), preheat the oven to 350°F. and place a rack in the center of the oven. Butter two 9-inch round cake pans. Lightly dust the sides of the pans with flour, tapping out the excess, and line the bottom with circles of parchment or waxed paper.

2. In a medium saucepan, cook the chile powder in 1 cup of the water over medium heat until simmering. Remove the pan from the heat, stir in the vanilla, and set aside.

3. Using a mixer with a wire whip attachment for best results, combine the flours, sugar, baking soda, salt, and cocoa and beat on low speed until well mixed. Add the softened butter to the dry mixture and beat thoroughly on medium-low speed. The mixture should be a uniform grainy texture. Raise the speed to medium and gradually add the remaining cup of water and the buttermilk. Add the eggs one at a time, beating well after each addition.

4. Slowly add the water/chile mixture and continue to beat just until well combined; be sure not to overbeat. Pour the mixture equally into the pans and bake for 35 to 40 minutes or until a toothpick inserted in the center of each layer comes out clean.

5. To cool, set the pans on a wire rack for 15 minutes. Then turn the cakes out onto the rack, remove the paper from the bottom, and immediately invert so that the risen tops don't flatten. Let sit until completely cool before frosting.

6. For the frosting, combine the butter and cocoa in a large saucepan and melt over medium heat. Stir in the buttermilk. Add the confectioners' sugar a little at a time, stirring with a wire whisk between additions. Stir in the bourbon and vanilla and continue to whisk until frosting is smooth and glossy. The frosting should stiffen as it cools. (In warm weather you may need to refrigerate it.) When it is still warm but has reached a spreadable consistency, you can assemble the cake.

7. If necessary, trim the tops of the cakes so that they are level. Place one of the cake layers on a 9-inch round cardboard cake circle. Spread 1 cup of the frosting over the layer. Sprinkle 1 cup of the chopped walnuts (if using) evenly over the frosting. Place the second layer of cake on the frosted base. Use the remaining frosting to cover the top and sides of the cake. Finish the top of the cake by holding the spatula at a slight angle and making several strokes to smooth the top. To decorate the cake, press the remaining walnuts onto the lower half of the sides and on top of the cake. This cake is best when made 1 to 2 days before serving, as it gives the flavors time to blend.

Bobbie's Cheesecake

Our family friend Bobbie Chaim introduced us to this delectable cheesecake—the creamiest, lightest, moistest slice of heaven you will ever put in your mouth! Bobbie used to bring one every Christmas as a gift for my father, and I couldn't keep out of the refrigerator where the leftovers were stored, slicing a sliver for a sinful late-night snack. The crust contains vanilla sugar, which Bobbie claims is the secret of Viennese baking. The tablespoon sprinkled over the cake before baking makes all the difference in the world. And using Philadelphia cream cheese is critical: Other packaged cream cheeses are too salty and fresh cream cheese does not contain the necessary stabilizers. The huckleberry preserves are the crowning glory. If you can't find them, substitute blueberry preserves. They are very similar.

SERVES 12

Ingredients

GERMAN MÜRBETEIG CRUST

1½ cups all-purpose flour

¾ teaspoon baking powder

⅓ cup sugar

Pinch of salt

1 tablespoon vanilla sugar (see Note)

1 large egg

8 tablespoons (1 stick) unsalted butter or margarine, softened

FILLING

4 large egg whites, at room temperature

1 cup vanilla sugar

¼ teaspoon pure vanilla extract

24 ounces Kraft Philadelphia cream cheese

TOPPING

1 pint sour cream

2 tablespoons vanilla sugar

½ teaspoon pure vanilla extract

Directions

1. Preheat the oven to 350°F.

2. For the crust: In a mixing bowl, combine the flour, baking powder, sugar, salt, and vanilla sugar. Add the egg and softened butter and mix until the dough forms a ball. This is easiest to do in a stand mixer with a dough hook attachment. Pat the dough into an 8-inch springform pan, lining the bottom and sides all the way to the top. Try to achieve a uniform thickness.

3. For the filling: Beat the egg whites until fairly stiff but not dry. Add the vanilla sugar slowly and then add the vanilla. Slowly, in small amounts, add the cream cheese. Mix to smooth the major lumps, but be careful not to overbeat. Pour into the crust-lined pan and bake on the middle rack of the oven for 25 minutes. Remove from the oven and set aside.

4. Raise the oven temperature to 500°F. While the oven is heating, prepare the topping. Combine the sour cream, vanilla sugar, and vanilla. Spread very gently on the top of the cheesecake and bake for 5 minutes. Let cool at room temperature and then refrigerate. Remove the springform pan and keep the cheesecake tightly covered with plastic wrap. Serve well chilled.

Note: To make vanilla sugar, place several vanilla beans in a tall jar. Pour sugar over the beans to nearly fill the jar. Shake it up a bit, then put the jar in your spice cabinet. After a week, you'll have lovely vanilla sugar. Simply replace the sugar with fresh sugar as you use it.

Bananas Flambé with Hudson's Bay Co. Rum

Bananas flambé may not seem like a typical Western dessert, but we put it on our menu when we first opened in 1963. It's so tasty and universally loved, why not? We used to flambé it with Hudson's Bay Company (HBC) 151-proof rum, which had such a high level of alcohol that the pan fired quickly and burned off the alcohol to leave behind the dark, luscious rum flavor—after a spectacular tableside show. In 1987 HBC sold its distilling operations to Seagram's; while you can't find HBC rum any longer, you can use Largo Bay 151 or Gosling's 151 Rum instead for a delicious outcome.

Hudson's Bay Company was once the largest landholder in North America, with most of its property in Canada. It was founded in 1670 and for many years prospered so successfully that by the early days of the 19th century it was a multimillion-dollar empire. In 1833, Bent, St. Vrain and Company in southern Colorado and the North American Fur Trade Company owned by John Jacob Astor were in head-to-head competition with HBC.

SERVES 4

Ingredients

4 bananas

4 tablespoons unsalted butter

2 tablespoons dark honey

Juice of 1 small lime

Dash of ground cinnamon

¼ cup 151-proof dark rum

Directions

1. Cut the bananas in half lengthwise, then in half crosswise, yielding 4 pieces per banana.

2. In a chafing dish, cook the butter, honey, lime juice, and cinnamon over high heat to boiling. Gently place the bananas in the chafing dish, flat side down. Lower the heat and simmer for 3 minutes, then add the rum. Light a match and carefully flame the dish. Coat the banana pieces well with sauce and serve 4 pieces to a plate. These may be arranged around a scoop of vanilla ice cream.

HOW TO FLAMBÉ

Pay attention to the bananas, cherries, peaches, or anything else you set afire by dousing it with alcohol—the flames can get quite high! This is dramatic, to be sure, but the flames might lick over anything flammable in the vicinity (a dishtowel, a potholder, your sleeve) and cause some trouble. When the initial flame subsides, a small blue flame will continue to burn for several seconds. This is when you should rotate the pan to expose the fruit to any more alcohol that might ignite and burn off. The goal is to keep the blue flame alive for as long as possible to caramelize the sugars in the alcohol, reduce any raw alcohol flavor, and entertain your guests.

Thomas Jefferson's Peach Flambé with Scotch Whisky

Peach flambé can be set alight with rum, but at The Fort we have always used Scotch whisky, and no one has complained! It's a lovely summertime dessert when the peaches are ripe, juicy, and sweet. Even better if you have homemade vanilla ice cream. It's a dessert with history, too, since the story goes that Thomas Jefferson learned of it on one of his trips to France and introduced it to this country.

SERVES 4

Ingredients

8 peach halves, peeled and pitted

½ cup unsalted butter

1 cup sugar

1 cup high-proof Scotch whisky

Pinch of cinnamon

Vanilla ice cream

Directions

1. In a medium saucepan, combine butter, cinnamon, and sugar over low heat just until butter melts and sugar dissolves. Add the peach halves cut side down and bring heat up to medium-low. Cover; let simmer for 10 minutes. Turn the peaches over and continue to simmer, uncovered, for another 4 to 5 minutes.

2. Add Scotch to the pan and let it warm for 10 seconds or so. Carefully ignite the alcohol fumes and let the flames die out naturally. To serve, place 2 peach halves in a bowl on top of good vanilla ice cream and drizzle with remaining syrup. Serve immediately.

THE NEVER-ENDING APPEAL OF ICE CREAM

During the first snowfall of the winter, my mother always sent us outside to fill a bowl with fresh, clean snow so that we could make snow ice cream. We rapidly mixed the snow with cream, sugar, vanilla, and chocolate syrup or cinnamon and happily spooned the mixture from the bowl. This was so exciting for my brother and me—the first taste of winter's snow.

I have read that as early as AD 65, Roman emperor Nero sent his slaves to the mountains to collect snow so that he could mix it with fruit and honey. Centuries later, Marco Polo allegedly brought a recipe for snow mixed with yak milk, for an early version of ice milk, home to Italy from China, and a few centuries later, Catherine de Medici introduced ice milk to France. Although Catherine was from Florence, she became queen of France in 1533, and the French, not content with the Italian version, reportedly added chocolate and strawberries to the icy dessert. Charles I of England is said to have taken ice cream to his country, and from there it was not long before it became popular in the New World. In America, both Thomas Jefferson and Dolley Madison were known for serving ice cream, the former at Monticello and the latter at her husband's inaugural ball in 1813. While some historians refute this information, I appreciate its charm and bigger message that throughout history people have been drawn to sweet, cold desserts.

The evolution of ice cream as we know it today follows the trajectory of the invention of refrigeration. Today, we think of ice cream as an all-American treat. Ice cream shops and supermarkets offer a staggering number of different flavors, one more tempting than the next. If you are an ice cream lover, it's a magnificent time to be alive!

One of my favorite ice cream desserts is a prickly pear sundae. It's not really a recipe, since you pour prickly pear syrup over vanilla ice cream and have at it, but I could not write this book without mentioning it. If you want to try it, you can buy prickly pear syrup in some specialty stores or order it online. (See "Where to Find It!")

Colorado Cherries Jamboree

Clearly, we liked flambéed desserts in the early days of The Fort, both because they taste good and because they are impressive to prepare at the table. Cherries from Colorado's Western Slope make a delicious cherry jamboree, which is also known as cherries jubilee.

SERVES 4–6

Ingredients

½ cup sugar

2 tablespoons cornstarch

¼ cup water

¼ cup orange juice

1 pound Bing or other dark, sweet cherries, rinsed and pitted, or 1 (16-ounce) package frozen pitted cherries

½ teaspoon finely grated orange zest

Vanilla ice cream

1 tablespoon cherry brandy or liqueur or ¼ teaspoon cherry extract

¼ cup cognac or brandy

Directions

1. Whisk together the sugar and cornstarch in a skillet or sauté pan. Stir in the water and orange juice; bring to a boil over medium-high heat, whisking until thickened. Stir in the cherries and orange zest, return to a boil, and then reduce the heat. Simmer for 6 to 8 minutes for fresh cherries, or 2 to 3 minutes for frozen cherries.

2. While the cherries are cooking, spoon the ice cream into serving bowls.

3. Remove the cherries from the heat and stir in the cherry brandy. Carefully ignite it using a long fireplace match. Gently shake the pan until the blue flame has extinguished itself. Spoon the cherries over the bowls of ice cream.

Holly's Adobe Brick Sundae

We serve a lot of ice cream sundaes at The Fort, including one I "invented" when I was 10 years old. I named it Holly's Adobe Brick Sundae. In those days, you could get a small brick of vanilla ice cream, which I put on a salad plate and sprinkled generously with a mixture of Nestlé's hot cocoa mix, sugar, and cinnamon before grabbing a spoon. As the ice cream melted, I stirred the dry mixture into the creamy liquid to create a sauce. My parents thought it was so innovative for a kid, they put it on the menu, where it has remained in one form or another to this day!

SERVES 6–8

Ingredients

1½ quarts vanilla ice cream

1 cup Nesquik or another sweetened chocolate milk mix

2 tablespoons raw or granulated sugar

1 teaspoon ground cinnamon

Lightly sweetened whipped cream, flavored with vanilla, for garnish

6–8 sprigs fresh mint, for garnish

Directions

1. Fill a small loaf pan (4½ x 9 inches) with slightly softened vanilla ice cream. Return to the freezer for several hours, until the ice cream has hardened.

2. In a small bowl, combine the chocolate mix, sugar, and cinnamon and set aside.

3. To serve: Run a thin-bladed kitchen knife around the inside edges of the loaf pan and invert the pan onto a cutting board. If the ice cream loaf doesn't unmold easily, place a clean dish towel soaked in cold water, and rung out, over the loaf pan to loosen the bottom, then lift off the pan. Dip the blade of the knife in cold water and cut 1½- to 2-inch-thick slices (bricks) off of the loaf.

4. Sprinkle the chocolate mixture over the ice cream. Garnish each serving with a dollop of whipped cream and a sprig of mint. Serve immediately.

Homemade Butterscotch Sundae

My husband, Jeremy, loves homemade butterscotch, and this is one of his favorite desserts. Spoon it over any flavor of ice cream you like.

SERVES 4–6

Ingredients

1 tablespoon corn syrup

About 2 tablespoons water

1½ teaspoons fresh lime juice

1½ cups sugar

Dusting of cream of tartar

1 cup heavy cream

3 tablespoons unsalted butter

1 quart vanilla bean ice cream

¼ cup pine nuts, lightly toasted

Whipped cream

Directions

1. In a medium saucepan, combine the corn syrup, water, and lime juice. (You may need less than 2 tablespoons of water; just cover the bottom of the saucepan.) Then, over medium heat, add the sugar and dust the cream of tartar lightly over the top of it. Do not stir! Just jiggle the pan occasionally. When the sugar is melted and a dark caramel color is achieved, 1 to 2 minutes later, turn off the heat.

2. Slowly whisk in the cream. When the cream is thoroughly mixed in, add the butter. Stir until the butter is melted. Return the sauce to the heat. Stirring constantly, bring it to a simmer. Once the simmer point is achieved, cook, stirring, for 60 seconds exactly. Remove from the heat and set the saucepan in an ice bath.

3. Place 2 scoops of ice cream in each sundae dish. Top with warm butterscotch sauce, a sprinkling of pine nuts, and a dollop of whipped cream. Serve immediately! The sauce may be made in advance, covered, and refrigerated for up to 1 week before serving. Bring it to room temperature or reheat.

Triple Cherry Cast-Iron Cobbler à la Mode

While this recipe is for cherries, we also make a cast-iron cobbler with apples and peaches, depending on the season and what fruit is at its peak. Cherries are at their best in the middle of the summer and so you can be pretty sure of finding this on our menu in July or August. We call it a "cast-iron" cobbler to reference the rustic desserts made in Dutch ovens set over campfires by the settlers who traveled west.

SERVES 4–6

Ingredients

STREUSEL TOPPING

⅔ cup all-purpose flour

⅓ cup old-fashioned oats

⅓ cup packed brown sugar

¼ cup slivered almonds

¼ teaspoon cinnamon

4 tablespoons cold, unsalted butter, cut into cubes

FILLING

1 (15¼-ounce) can pitted Bing cherries in syrup (not prethickened)

1 (14½-ounce) can pitted tart cherries or fresh tart cherries (not pie filling)

½ cup black or red cherry nectar or juice

⅓ cup sugar

½ teaspoon salt

1 cup sun-dried cherries

¼ cup cornstarch, mixed with water to a thin paste

Directions

1. To make the streusel topping: In a mixing bowl, stir together the flour, oats, sugar, almonds, and cinnamon. Using a pastry blender, cut the butter into the dry ingredients until the mixture resembles coarse crumbs. Cover and chill the streusel until ready to use.

2. Preheat the oven to 375°F.

3. Strain the two types of canned cherries, saving the juice. Mix the reserved juices, cherry nectar, sugar, and salt together in a medium saucepan and bring to a boil. Place the canned and dried cherries in an 8- to 9-inch cast-iron skillet or a 9-inch shallow baking dish. When the mixture comes to a boil, stir in the cornstarch mixture. Reduce the heat to medium and cook, stirring, for 3 to 5 minutes, until the juices thicken. Pour the juices over the cherries, and top with the streusel. Bake the cobbler for about 30 minutes or until golden brown. Let sit for 30 minutes before serving.

Sarah's Rosemary-Infused Panna Cotta

This rosemary-kissed custard was created by our pastry chef, Sarah Bailey, who makes everything with love and passion. I particularly like to watch her work because her devotion and care are evident in every movement. One of my personal favorites, this light, creamy, and eggless Italian-style dessert is best when it is served the same day you make it.

SERVES 4–6

Ingredients

1½ teaspoons unflavored gelatin

2 cups heavy cream

6 tablespoons sugar

2 sprigs fresh rosemary

6 ounces fresh huckleberries or blueberries

Lightly sweetened whipped cream

Directions

1. Soften the gelatin in 1 tablespoon of cold water.

2. In a medium saucepan, combine the cream and sugar. Add the rosemary sprigs and place over medium heat until the cream reaches a simmer. Remove the cream from the heat and allow it to steep for 5 minutes.

3. Remove and discard the rosemary and stir in the gelatin. Stir until the gelatin is melted and well incorporated. Pour the mixture into wineglasses or ramekins and chill for 3 hours.

4. Top each panna cotta with fresh berries and whipped cream.

Montana's Wild Huckleberry Crème Brûlée

This is another creation from our talented pastry chef, Sarah Bailey, who makes smooth, creamy crème brûlée, with its characteristic and irresistible crispy topping of caramelized sugar, according to the season. We have put cinnamon, coffee, and pumpkin brûlée on the menu, but this wild huckleberry dessert is hands-down our customers' favorite.

SERVES 4–6

Ingredients

2 cups (1 pint) heavy whipping cream

4 large egg yolks

½ cup sugar

1 teaspoon pure vanilla extract

1 cup Huckleberry preserves (see "Where to Find It!") or blueberry preserves

¾ cup raw sugar

Directions

1. Preheat the oven to 300°F.

2. Pour the cream into a large saucepan.

3. Separate the eggs. Place the yolks in a medium mixing bowl and reserve the whites for another use. Add ½ cup sugar to the yolks and whisk until the mixture turns pale yellow. Over medium heat, bring the cream just to a simmer. Gradually whisk the hot cream into the yolks.

4. Spread a thin layer of huckleberry preserves in the bottom of 4 to 6 ramekins. Fill the ramekins with the cream mixture. Place the ramekins in a shallow roasting pan and add enough hot water to come about halfway up the sides. Bake for 1 hour or until the custard is barely set. Place the ramekins in another shallow roasting pan and pour in enough cold water to come halfway up the sides. When cool, refrigerate the custards until completely set.

5. To serve, lightly sprinkle raw sugar over the top of each custard and place the custards under a hot broiler for a few seconds to caramelize the sugar. If you often make crème brûlée, you may want to invest in a special butane chef's torch made for caramelizing sugar.

Capirotada "Spotted Dog" Bread Pudding

This bread pudding evolved from the old Spanish dish called capirotada, which, according to *Libro del Arte de Cozina*, a cookbook compiled by Diego Granado in the late 1500s, began as a savory dish of layered bread, onions, cheese, and meat or poultry. It was topped with sweet meringue, an odd flourish to our modern sensibilities. My father conjectured that a dessert similar to this originated in New Mexico in the early 19th century, when it showed up in various journals and histories.

"It is quite likely that the many apple orchards of New Mexico grew from seeds brought from Europe in the very early days by French and Spanish priests, when a supply wagon train came from Mexico to the missions every two years," Dad wrote. "Later, more frequent wagon trains continued to bring wines, fruit, grape shoots, chocolate, cheeses, and delicacies north to New Mexico." He continued to explain that the dessert was considered a Lenten dish in New Mexico and further south in Mexico. "Onions in a dessert may seem strange," he conjectured, "but when cooked, they add to the pleasing apple flavor." As to its name, Dad said it was often called "spotted dog" because of the raisins, and because the mountain men "had little patience with the Spanish language."

SERVES 6

Ingredients

1½ cups crushed piloncillo or brown sugar

1 cup water

½ medium sweet yellow onion, finely chopped

3 large eggs

1½ cups half-and-half or whole milk

4 cups toasted bread, cut or torn into approximately 1½-inch pieces

¾ cup sultana raisins (plumped in hot water if too dry)

1 Gala or Granny Smith apple, peeled, cored, quartered, and sliced

4 tablespoons unsalted butter or margarine

1½ teaspoons ground cinnamon

½ teaspoon grated nutmeg

1 cup grated yellow cheddar cheese

Heavy cream, for pouring on top

Directions

1. Preheat the oven to 350°F.

2. In a small saucepan, boil the sugar and water on the stove over medium heat, for 5-10 minutes, or until the sugar is completely dissolved and it has reduced down to a syrup. Add the onion and continue boiling for 5 minutes.

3. In a separate bowl, stir together the eggs and half-and-half. Don't beat them!

4. In a 3-quart baking dish, layer the bread, raisins, apple, butter, cinnamon, and nutmeg. Pour the syrup-onion mixture on top, then the egg-milk mixture. Push down the filling with a spoon to make sure all the ingredients become moist.

5. Bake for 40 minutes, remove from the oven, and spread the grated cheese on top. Return the pudding to the oven for 5 minutes or until the cheese is melted and well browned. The pudding should absorb all the liquid and be very moist, with a well-browned top. If it seems to be getting too brown, cover with foil for the remainder of the cooking time. Serve hot with a bit of cold heavy cream poured over each serving.

Note: Capirotada may be baked ahead of time, except for the cheese topping. Thirty minutes before serving, preheat the oven to 350°F. Cover the capirotada and heat for 20 minutes. Top with the cheese and return to the oven for 5 minutes to allow the cheese to melt and brown.

Charlie Carrillo's Natillas

Natillas is a traditional dessert in Mexico and New Mexico at Christmastime and resembles the dessert some call "floating island." The secret is to beat the egg whites until stiff, fold some into the custard, and then layer the rest with the custard for a light-as-air dessert. My friend Charlie Carrillo shared this recipe with me, and it's the best I have tasted.

While Charlie is a talented cook, his true gift is as a santero, a carver and painter of images of saints. He is recognized as one of the primary authorities on santero and as the most accomplished artist practicing the regional tradition. He has won the Museum of International Folk Art's Hispanic Heritage Award, as well as numerous prizes (usually first place) at the annual Traditional Spanish Market in Santa Fe. At the Tesoro Cultural Center, he helped me create our juried annual Spanish market by bringing award-winning santeros as well as tin makers, potters, and jewelers to the event. I greatly admire Charlie for his humility, devotion, and great sense of humor.

SERVES 6

Ingredients

2½ cups whole milk, divided

3 large egg yolks

⅓ cup sugar

1½ tablespoons cornstarch

1 teaspoon pure vanilla extract

Pinch of salt

3 pasteurized egg whites (see Note)

¼ teaspoon cream of tartar

3 tablespoons confectioners' sugar

Ground cinnamon and/or grated nutmeg

Directions

1. Pour 2¼ cups of the milk into the top of a double boiler and whisk in the egg yolks and sugar.

2. In a small bowl, combine the remaining ¼ cup of milk and the cornstarch to make a thin paste.

3. Fill the lower half of the double boiler with enough hot water to almost touch the bottom of the top pot. Gently cook the custard over medium-low heat, stirring constantly. Just before it begins to simmer, stir in the cornstarch mixture. Continue to stir for 10 to 15 minutes, until the custard thickens enough to thickly coat the back of a spatula. Remove the top pot from the heat and stir in the vanilla and salt. Set aside.

4. Place the egg whites in the bowl of an electric mixer and beat until soft peaks form. Add the cream of tartar and confectioners' sugar, and continue to beat until the meringue is stiff and glossy.

5. Layer one-third of the meringue in a shallow serving bowl. Pour in half of the hot custard, then layer with one-third of the meringue, the remaining custard, and a top layer of meringue. Gently fold the entire mixture one or two times. Do not overmix the layers. Refrigerate for 1 hour.

6. Sprinkle with cinnamon and/or nutmeg and serve chilled. The texture of this custard is best when it is eaten the day that you make it.

Note: Because of concerns about salmonella in some raw eggs, pasteurized egg whites are now sold at many supermarkets. We use them at The Fort when preparing uncooked meringue.

Bird's Nest Pudding

This recipe is one I remember from my childhood, and to this day I make it every Easter with the kids from my neighborhood. It calls for dozens of empty eggshells to use as molds, so I suggest you start collecting them a few weeks before you want to make this pudding, or plan on a lot of omelets. As with so many of the dishes I love, I learned this one from my father, Sam'l. Here is what he said about the pudding.

Easter wasn't Easter at our house when I was a child without Bird's Nest Pudding. I have no idea where my mother learned the dish. It probably came from her mother's English Quaker ancestors, the Fox family. I found a similar recipe with the same name in Brigg's Cookery, *published in London in 1788.*

It's basically a flavored blancmange molded in the shape of eggs and laid in a nest of candied orange and grapefruit strips on a bed of tasty wine gelatin. It's lots of fun for guests to choose which color egg they want. As a boy, I loved all of them, especially the green mint, blue almond, and pale vanilla.

MAKES 12 CUSTARD EGGS; SERVES 6

Ingredients

EGGSHELLS

1 dozen large eggs

WINE GELATIN

2 tablespoons unflavored gelatin

½ cup cold water

1⅔ cups boiling water

1 cup sugar

cup orange juice

1 cup wine (sweet sherry or Madeira or any sweet wine)

3 tablespoons fresh lemon juice

BLANCMANGE

2½ cups whole milk, scalded

1⅓ cups sugar

1 tablespoon cornstarch

1 teaspoon pure vanilla extract

Pinch of salt, or to taste

2 tablespoons unflavored gelatin

½ cup cold water

FOUR FLAVORS

½ teaspoon pure vanilla extract

2 drops yellow food coloring

½ teaspoon mint extract

2 drops green food coloring

½ teaspoon almond extract

2 drops blue food coloring

1 teaspoon unsweetened cocoa

CANDIED ORANGE PEEL

2 cups orange or grapefruit peel (no white pith), cut into thin strips

2 cups water, divided

2¾ cups sugar, divided

TOPPING

1 pint heavy cream

Directions

1. To prepare the eggshells: Pierce the eggs at the large end, carefully breaking a hole ½ to ¾ inch in diameter. Gently shake the white and yolk out through the hole into a mixing bowl. Use the eggs for scrambled eggs, quiche, or another egg recipe. Rinse out the shells and invert them onto paper towels to dry.

2. To make the wine gelatin: Sprinkle the gelatin on the cold water and let it soften according to the package instructions. Add the boiling water, sugar, orange juice, wine, and lemon juice. Stir until the sugar is dissolved. Fill a large, shallow serving bowl one-half to two-thirds full of the wine gelatin and chill for 3 to 5 hours, until set.

3. To make the blancmange: Whisk together the milk, sugar, cornstarch, vanilla, and salt in the top of a double boiler. Fill the bottom pot with enough hot water to almost reach the bottom of the top pot. Place the double boiler over medium heat and cook, stirring with a wooden spatula, until the mixture thickens enough to coat the back of the spatula. Sprinkle the gelatin over the cold water and let it soften according to the package instructions. Add to the hot blancmange and stir well.

4. To make the flavors: Divide the mixture equally among four bowls and stir in the ingredients to make different colored and flavored eggs: In one bowl, add the vanilla and yellow food coloring. In another bowl, add the mint flavoring and green food coloring. In the third bowl, add the almond extract and blue food coloring. Add cocoa powder to the fourth bowl.

5. Rinse the eggshells with cold water to moisten and carefully pour in the colored and flavored blancmange. Return the eggshells to the carton with the open end up and chill until set, at least 3 hours.

6. To candy the peel: While the eggs and gelatin are chilling, prepare the candied peel. Place the peel in a saucepan with 1⅓ cups cold water and bring to a boil. Simmer for 15 minutes, drain, and set aside.

7. Place 2 cups of sugar and ⅓ cup water in a saucepan and bring to a boil, swirling the pan to melt the sugar. Boil, swirling, until the syrup reaches the firm-ball stage (244°F on a candy thermometer). Immediately drop the strips of peel into the syrup and boil for 1 to 2 minutes, until the syrup has thickened. Remove the citrus strips with a slotted spoon and allow them to cool; then roll them in the remaining ¾ cup sugar.

8. To serve: When the gelatin has set, build a "nest" of citrus strips around the edge of a small dessert bowl and spoon wine gelatin into the middle. When you're ready to serve, carefully crack and peel 2 custard eggs per bowl and set them on the wine gelatin so that they look as if they are in a nest. Serve with heavy cream.

Beatriz's Flan

Flans are as popular in Mexico as in their native Spain and have immigrated to New Mexico, where a lot of the population is of Hispanic heritage. Made from easy-to-find and inexpensive ingredients (milk, eggs, sugar), the custards are soothingly smooth and pleasingly sweet. Flans must be cooked slowly at low heat because, if not, they will bubble and turn spongy.

This amazing recipe comes from Beatriz Molina, who was our baker for several years. Beatriz and her husband, Carlos, came to work at The Fort in 1986 from Argentina and lived on the top floor of the building for more than 25 years. Carlos was our maintenance manager, and when he died in 2009, he was laid to rest under the same pine tree next to our red rock as my father and mother; brother, Keith; pet bear, Sissy; and German shepherd, Lobo.

SERVES 8

Ingredients

6 large egg yolks

1 tablespoon pure vanilla extract

1 (14-ounce) can sweetened condensed milk

1 (12-ounce) can evaporated milk

1 cup whole milk

1½ cups sugar

Directions

1. Preheat the oven to 325°F. Mix together the egg yolks and vanilla, then add the condensed, evaporated, and fresh milk. Stir, don't beat, because beating will add air and result in a spongy flan.

2. Melt the sugar in a nonstick skillet, stirring almost constantly, until it becomes liquid and medium caramel in color. Watch it carefully! It will clump at first, then begin to melt. As the sugar melts, fill flan cups with very hot water. As soon as the sugar has caramelized, pour out the water from each cup, one at a time, and coat with caramel. Do this quickly. The syrup will harden almost instantly, and if it heats for even 30 seconds too long, it will turn to candy.

3. Fill the cups with the flan mixture and place them in a shallow roasting pan. Pour in enough boiling water to come halfway up the sides of the cups. Bake on the middle rack of the oven for 45 minutes or until the custard is set.

4. Remove the cups of flan from the oven, cool in a pan of ice water, and then refrigerate, preferably overnight, to allow the caramel to liquefy. When you're ready to serve it, run a knife around the edge of the cup, place a plate upside down on top of it, and invert it, so that the flan falls onto the plate, topped with the caramel.

Queso Napolitano

We have served this flan at The Fort for years. It's not always on the menu but is never absent for long. In the early 1950s, my father and mother read about a Mexico City restaurant in *Gourmet* magazine, and when they traveled there they discovered this creamy dessert.

SERVES 10–12

Ingredients

⅔ cup sugar

¼ cup water

1 (14-ounce) can sweetened condensed milk

1 (12-ounce) can evaporated milk

6 large eggs

1 tablespoon pure vanilla extract

8 ounces cream cheese

Directions

1. Preheat the oven to 325°F. Combine the sugar and water in a saucepan and cook over high heat, swirling the pot by the handle, to dissolve the sugar. When it comes to a boil, lower the heat to medium-low and simmer, swirling the pan often, until the sugar turns golden and caramelizes, 5 to 8 minutes. Once the sugar begins to caramelize, immediately pour the caramelized sugar into a flan mold and tilt so that it covers the bottom of the mold.

2. In the bowl of an electric mixer, combine the sweetened condensed milk, evaporated milk, eggs, vanilla, and cream cheese. Beat at medium speed until smooth.

3. Pour the mixture into the mold and cover with foil. Place the mold in another pan and pour in enough hot water to reach within an inch of the mold's top.

4. Bake for 40 to 50 minutes or until a knife inserted in the center of the custard comes out clean. Allow the flan to cool, then refrigerate overnight before unmolding and serving.

President Andrew Jackson's Trifle

We first made this trifle in 1996 for the 150th anniversary celebration of Charles Bent's appointment as governor of New Mexico. Bent's Fort was built in 1833, during the last full year of Andrew Jackson's term as president. Jackson had a renowned sweet tooth and reportedly was extremely fond of this pudding made with sherry-soaked macaroons, sherry-flavored whipped cream, and orange marmalade. We serve this for private parties, always to great acclaim.

SERVES 8–10

Ingredients

2 cups whole milk

⅓ cup sugar

Pinch of salt

1½ tablespoons cornstarch

2 large eggs

½ teaspoon almond extract

½ pound almond macaroons

½ cup sweet sherry

1 cup orange or grapefruit marmalade

TOPPING

½ pint heavy whipping cream

2 teaspoons sugar

1 teaspoon sweet sherry

½ cup slivered almonds, toasted

Directions

1. In a saucepan over medium heat, bring the milk to a simmer.

2. Place the sugar, salt, cornstarch, and eggs in the top of a double boiler. Beat until smooth, then whisk in the hot milk a little at a time.

3. Fill the bottom pot with enough hot water to almost reach the bottom of the top pot. Place the double boiler over medium heat and cook, stirring with a wooden spatula, until the custard has the consistency of mayonnaise. Remove the custard from the heat and stir in the almond extract. Set aside to cool.

5. Arrange the macaroons on the bottom of a glass serving bowl. Pour ½ cup sherry over them, and then cover with the custard. Spread the marmalade on the top.

6. To make the topping, beat the heavy cream, sugar, and 1 teaspoon sherry until the cream stands in peaks. Top the trifle with the whipped cream and garnish with the almond slivers. Chill before serving.

Green Chile Ice Cream

When I was experimenting with different flavors of ice cream, I discovered that if I rinsed canned green chiles and added them to the mixture, they tasted almost like pineapple after they were processed in the ice cream machine. I started with the avocado ice cream my dad had made for an old television show called *Frying Pans West*, so I guess you could say this ice cream is a joint venture between Dad and me.

SERVES 2

Ingredients

2 ripe avocados

Juice of 1 lime

1 cup confectioners' sugar

1 (8-ounce) can mild green chiles, rinsed, patted dry, and coarsely chopped

1½ cups whipped cream or vanilla ice cream

1 mint sprig, for garnish

Directions

1. Peel and slice the avocados. Transfer the avocado flesh to the bowl of an electric mixer bowl with the lime juice and confectioners' sugar. With the mixer on low speed, beat the mixture until smooth. Add the green chiles and mix until incorporated. Add the whipped cream or ice cream and beat until thoroughly mixed.

2. Transfer the mixture to an ice cream machine and freeze according to the manufacturer's instructions. Serve garnished with mint.

Where to Find It!

Aluminum Foil Smoking Bags

Camerons
1660 S. Circle Dr.
Colorado Springs, CO 80910
(719) 390-0505
www.cameronsproducts.com

Buffalo Tongue and Buffalo Marrow Bones

Mohawk Bison
47 Allyn Rd.
Goshen, CT 06756
(860) 201-7550
www.mohawkbison.com

Northstar Bison
222 Birch Ave.
Cameron, WI 54822
(715) 458-4300
www.northstarbison.com

Curry Bush Leaves

iShopIndian.com
10701 W. North Ave.
Wauwatosa, WI 53226
(877) 786-8876
www.ishopindian.com

Dried Damiana

San Francisco Herb Company
250 14th St.
San Francisco, CA 94103
(800) 227-4530
www.sfherb.com

Grits

Southern Grace Farms
3131 Vickers Church Rd.
Enigma, GA 31749
(229) 533-8585
www.southerngracefarms.com

Heirloom Beans

Adobe Milling Company
60740 Hwy. 491
Dove Creek, CO 81324
(800) 542-3623, (970) 677-2620
www.anasazibeans.com

Purcell Mountain Farms
393 Firehouse Rd.
Moyie Springs, ID 83845
(208) 267-0627
www.purcellmountainfarms.com

Rancho Gordo
1924 Yajome St.
Napa, CA 94559
(800) 599-8323, (707) 259-1935
www.ranchogordo.com

Huckleberry Preserves

The Huckleberry Patch Gift Shop
8868 US Hwy. 2 East
Hungry Horse, MT 59919
(800) 527-7340
www.huckleberrypatch.com

Larchwood Farms
3430 E. Seltice Way
Port Falls, ID 83854
(208) 762-1150
www.larchwoodfarms.com

Lamb Spareribs

Lava Lake Lamb
215 N. Main St.
Hailey, ID 83333
(888) 528-5253, (208) 788-1710
www.lavalakelamb.com

Rafter W Ranch
27178 State Hwy. 86
Simla, CO 80832
(719) 541-1002
www.rafterwranch.net

Prickly Pear Syrup

Cheri's Desert Harvest
1840 E. Winsett St.
Tucson, AZ 85719
(800) 743-1141, (520) 623-4141
www.cherisdesertharvest.com

CHAR CRUST
3017 N. Lincoln Ave.
Chicago, IL 60657
1-800-311-9884
www.charcrust.com

Index

About the Author

Holly Arnold Kinney is a Colorado entrepreneur and both the author and the publisher of *Shinin' Times at The Fort* (2010); *Sam Arnold's Frying Pans West* (2011), a companion cookbook to the PBS series; and a young reader's book, *Sissy Bear at The Fort* (2016).

Kinney lived at The Fort with her family starting in 1963 and worked in the restaurant as well as in the national advertising agency her parents owned. In 1981 she founded Arnold Media Services, an international advertising and public relations firm specializing in the gourmet food industry. In 1999 Kinney downsized her public relations company and joined her father in partnership in The Fort business. In 2006 Kinney's father passed away and she purchased the remaining business and property.

Kinney currently is actively running The Fort with the 90 employees she refers to as her "Fort family." She also is the founder and executive director of a nonprofit foundation, the Tesoro Cultural Center.

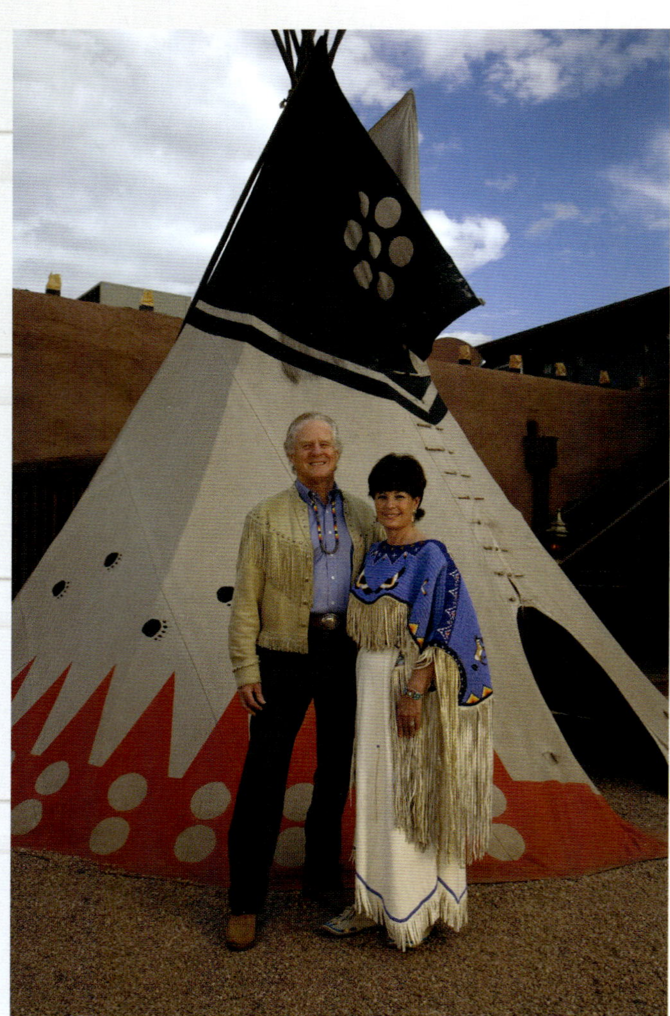